C000135991

Coast of Conflict

THE STORY OF THE SOUTH KENT COAST

Michael & Martin George

S.B. Publications

Dedicated to Harry George
2nd Bn. Oxfordshire and Buckinghamshire Light Infantry
who fell at the Battle of Loos on the 25th September 1915

First published in 2004 by S.B. Publications
19 Grove Road, Seaford, East Sussex BN25 1TP

ISBN 1 85 770 297 2

Typeset by EH Graphics, East Sussex (01273) 515527
Printed and bound by Ethos Productions Ltd.

*Cover illustrations are from watercolour paintings by Captain William Henry Ford, R.E., designer of
the Martello Towers. Painted in 1810, they show Tower number 4 and the view across Sandgate to Hythe
Bay and Romney Marsh in the distance. Reproduced by kind permission of William Drummond ©.*

conditions and a substantial increase in the size of Shorncliffe army camp. These improved facilities were to prove so important with the outbreak of the First World War, when the area became home to many thousands of British, Empire and Canadian troops on their way to the Western Front. Folkestone and Hythe were very much on the front line; the guns at Ypres could be heard, the wounded arrived in increasing numbers and, in 1917, death and destruction rained from the skies.

With the help of diaries, records and anecdotes we shall follow the fortunes of this corner of Kent during a century of war and peace; from Napoleon to the Armistice in 1918, looking at the relationships between the military and civilian communities. Folkestone, Hythe and Sandgate and surrounding villages have been 'home' to countless thousands of soldiers over the years. Some chose to stay and raise a family, some returned to their native lands, perhaps having married a local lass. For others the towns were little more than a brief halt en route to some foreign conflict from which far too many did not return.

In its own way, Shorncliffe Military Cemetery is a microcosm of military life over the last two centuries. With practically every regiment in the British Army represented, it reflects the activities at the nearby camp. It is a small cemetery when compared with many of those maintained by the Commonwealth War Graves Commission, but it has many stories of its own to tell.

There are no longer any barracks in Hythe, although the Small Arms School Corps still proudly takes advantage of its Freedom of the town by exercising the right to march along the High Street with bayonets fixed. Folkestone, on the other hand, remains an active garrison town and is proud to be home to the UK based battalion of the Brigade of Ghurkhas. The sound of gunfire from Hythe ranges and surrounding training grounds can often be heard and the people of Folkestone and Hythe, as did their forbears, can still enjoy open days at Shorncliffe camp where they are entertained by the music and skills of the men and traditional Nepalese dancing by their wives.

Many of the features described in this book still exist and are freely accessible to the public. There are several Martello Towers still standing, and some of them are open to visitors. The Royal Military Canal is world famous and its enjoyment has been enhanced by the cinder track laid down in 2002. There are also a considerable number of other, less well known, memorials to the past.

For those who would point out that we have omitted to mention the many other Napoleonic defences around the Kent, and indeed, the British coast, we acknowledge that to be the case. The east coast Martello Towers, the London defences, the polygonal forts and Dover Castle are all dealt with adequately elsewhere. If justification for this approach should be needed we find it (perhaps with tongue-in-cheek) in the words of the Hythe and Sandgate Guide, published in 1809,

> This part of the island, being most contiguous to the parts
> of the continent which are possessed by our ancient

enemies, the natural beauty of its scenery hath from time to time obtained embellishments from the hands of art, and in consequence of the present formidable and threatening posture of this wilful and inveterate foe, the whole range of shore between these highlands and the sea, are now occupied with castellated batteries of cannon, a vast military canal, and large military roads, the whole of which are protected with breastworks, entrenchments and every species of defensive preparation, completing the most gratifying view this country boasts, and is a grand illustration of the power, capacity and genius of its inhabitants.

The approach we have adopted is also the same for later time periods in the book; we have retained our geographical focus, preferring to move through time rather than space.

We hope that you enjoy reading this book, whether your interest is local, military or social history. If we have stirred an interest in the events and places that make up the Coast of Conflict, you will find our website, www.coastofconflict.com, a useful companion to the book. It gives details of recommended walks, contains many pictures and stories that did not find their way into the book, and a selection of useful links. And finally, if you would like to contact us with stories, suggestions or information, we would love to hear from you. Our publishers would be happy to forward any mail or email us directly at: martin@coastofconflict.com or michael@coastofconflict.com.

Chapter 1

FRANCE DECLARES WAR ON ENGLAND

The French Revolution had been watched by the British with a mixture of alarm and admiration until the French King, Louis XVI, had been marched by the Paris mob to *Madame Guillotine* on January 21st 1793. To a nation fiercely loyal to its own monarch, the slightly mad George III, such behaviour was unforgivable. Two weeks later the French Republic declared war on England and, for the next decade or more, the country was braced for the expected invasion of her shores. During the closing years of the eighteenth century the number of doomed attempts by the French to mount invasions at different points of the British Isles was matched only by the inglorious military forays by the British onto mainland Europe. In essence, a standoff had been reached, with Britain ruling the seas but with France the masters of continental Europe.

Napoleon Bonaparte. For twenty years he dreamed of invading Britain and 'avenging 600 years of insults'.

As early as October 1797 France's revolutionary ruling Directory had ordered the immediate assembly of an army for the purpose of invading England. In command of this Army of England was a young General, a rising star in the French military; his name was Bonaparte. Following a tour of the channel coast in February 1798, Bonaparte issued an order showing that he intended Boulogne to be his centre of operations, and the south Kent coast to be the object of the planned invasion:

DUNKIRK 12th February 1798.

General Caffarelli will repair at once to Boulogne and take measures for the improvement of the harbour; it must be capable of accommodating 50 gunboats...; one or two divisions of horse transports; six ships of 100 tons for the Staff; six ships for artillery; six ships for the official management; six ships for hospitals.

He will inspect the batteries defending Boulogne, and increase them if necessary...he will send privateers with an engineer officer to reconnoitre the English coast from Folkestone to Rye, to ascertain the real conditions of defence on that part of the coast, and to take note of the batteries which it would be necessary to carry, or take by surprise, so as to effect a landing.

BONAPARTE.

If the French had launched an invasion at this early stage in hostilities the outcome would have been disastrous for Britain. The security of the British Isles rested, as it had done for generations, on the Royal Navy's mastery of the high seas but, if the enemy had been able to give the Channel Fleet the slip and land on our shores, the defenders would have been hard pressed. Home defence rested largely with the county Militias, a ragtag army of men, conscripted by ballot to serve for five years. Ill-trained, ill-disciplined and ill-equipped they would have been no match for the French invasion army. In 1794 the British government, in answer to this crisis, passed the Volunteer Act allowing men to *voluntarily enrol themselves for the defence of their counties, towns and coasts, or for the general defence of the kingdom during the present war.* By 1801, over 400,000 men had signed up.

This Napoleonic 'Dad's Army' of part time soldiers were plentiful and keen, but they would have needed more than numbers and spirit to face the battle hardened soldiers of France. First in their list of needs were arms and ammunition, both of which were in short supply. Many of the volunteers were armed with nothing more lethal than pitchforks and scythes, a fact which was not lost on the editor of The Thrasher:

> Thus, while I work, and laugh, and sing,
> And at my thrashing toil,
> Unless I'm call'd on by my King,
> To guard my native soil:
> Then, accustom'd to thrashing, I'll swing round the flail,
> And thrash the proud foes to secure my brown ale.

John Bull on his way to fight for King and Country. One of many illustrations by James Gillray produced throughout the Napoleonic period.

Some volunteers made use of their own fowling pieces, weapons of doubtful reliability. For those few who could afford to equip themselves properly, enterprising traders were offering to sell warranted firelocks at £2 each. The government was unprepared for the tidal wave of volunteers; local units were springing up, so it seemed, on every street corner and village green. Regulations were hurriedly issued containing 'hints' and 'suggestions' on the positioning of barricades, and the provision of hand grenades to inhabitants of houses at road junctions.

The towns along the south Kent coast had rallied to the call for volunteers. First, troops of yeomanry cavalry were formed, including those at Lydd and Elham. Together with those from other local towns, they became the East Kent Yeomanry Cavalry. These volunteers had to provide their own horse and clothing, so membership tended to be fairly exclusive. The humble worker, cast in the same mould as the indomitable John Bull, was unlikely to find a place in the yeomanry, where the conditions of service reflected that 'these Troops of Cavalry to serve during the war were to consist of gentlemen and yeomen and such persons as they shall bring forward to be approved of by the Lord Lieutenant under authority of His Majesty.' There were, however, other opportunities for John Bull; he could join the infantry volunteers. The towns of New Romney, Lydd, Hythe and Folkestone had all been busy recruiting men, and these were all brought under the umbrella of the Cinque Ports Volunteers. Meticulous efforts were made to establish the number of men capable of bearing arms. The returns for Folkestone listed "all males of sufficient age to bring anything into the field, and of every weapon they possessed, from a spade or a shovel, to a sword or a gun."

The Volunteers took their work seriously, donning their uniforms and practising drill at every spare moment. Despite their improvisations, these men were seen as a serious defensive option in the event of invasion. The country was on permanent alert, but it was in 1798 that things reached a head. There had been three abortive attempts by the French to land in Ireland; would the next attempt be along the coast of Kent? The pastor of Lyminge church must have literally put the fear of God into his flock, by suggesting that "perhaps before the next Sunday dawns upon us, we might cease to be an independent nation." Even as the congregation left church, they were reminded of the brooding menace across the Channel; posters were pinned to every village oak and lych-gate, with just one word printed in stark type: INVASION. Although the French did not arrive that year, the parades and drills continued for the Volunteers. On the 24th July 1801 a General Order was issued from the District Headquarters at Dover Castle,

Keep practising. These cartoons poked mild fun at the Volunteers. The Georgians enjoyed the 'double entendre'!

FROM the great force now collecting on the coast of France, it is probable the Enemy may have a rashness to presume to attempt a Descent upon Kent and Sussex. The Yeomanry and Volunteer Corps, in the Southern District, will hold themselves in constant readiness to assemble at

their respective places of Parade, on the first Information
of the Enemy's appearance off the Coast.

Being a Volunteer, however, was not all spit and polish. In a county which had
forced terms with William the Conqueror, the Men of Kent were not going to be
intimidated by the 'rascals' on the other side of the Channel. They found time to
compose and sing dozens of stirring camp-fire songs telling of the fate which
awaited the would-be invaders. The following are verses from just two of these:

The Kent Volunteers
By T.H., A Trooper
Sound the Trumpet, and call out your soldiers to arms,
Whose bosoms true old English liberty warms,
See France rears her head, and with furey appears,
Let her come, we're prepared with the Kent Volunteers.
fol de rol

Shall French Men our spirits of freedom subdue,
Plant Guillotines where Liberty grew,
Our King to destroy with what'er we hold dear?
Bravely die each Briton and Kent Volunteers.

The above song, which had a total of seven verses, was to be sung to the
rollicking tune of *'Gee ho Dobbin!'* Unfortunately, we have been unable to find the
score for that old favourite. The next song was composed in 1794, and contains six
verses. It exults not only the Volunteers on land, but also the Royal Navy which,
under Admiral Howe, had secured the Channel that year, on the 'Glorious First
of June':

A Song

When Men of Kent protect our coast,
We scorn the threat'ning hostile host,
And freely cast away our fears,
Whilst guarded by such Volunteers.

Sedition foul shall hide its head,
And lurking Treason vengeance dread,
Since loyal Kent now proudly rears
Her brave, her gallant Volunteers.

These and a host of other patriotic numbers would have echoed around Mote

Park, near Maidstone, at a remarkable event held on the 1st August, 1799. This was the seat of the Lord Lieutenant of Kent, Lord Romney, and he decided to throw a party for six thousand of the county's volunteers. Also in attendance was King George III and most of the Royal family, together with William Pitt, the Prime Minister, and other members

Party in the Park 1799. 6000 Volunteers were entertained by Lord Romney at Mote Park near Maidstone. The Royal Family was also there. From a colour aquatint by William Alexander. (PM)

of the government. The spectacle of what has been described as the biggest picnic of all time drew a crowd of twenty thousand onlookers.

In addition to the cavalry and infantry volunteers the coast was defended by an array of artillery. As a Cinque Port, Hythe had been one of the first towns in England to be equipped with cannons. Hasted, in his History of Kent, described the town's defences at the end of the eighteenth century,

> Here is a small fort, of six guns, for the protection of the town and fishery, which till lately belonged to the town, which was bought by the Government but now rendered useless by its distance from the sea (somewhat more than half a mile) from the land continuing to gain upon it: the guns have been lately taken out.

But the guns soon returned; the threat of invasion meant that the stretch of coast between Dungeness and Folkestone became one of the most heavily fortified in England. The four batteries of Lade Fort were built at Dungeness, covering the anchorage and the beaches. Forts Moncrieff and Sutherland, to the west of Hythe each mounted eight 24-pound guns, while to the east of the town, on the site now occupied by the Hotel Imperial, stood Twiss Fort. In 1803 this fort mounted six 24-pounders, and these were joined in 1805 by two carronades, capable of pulverising enemy ships with their massive shot. On the hills overlooking Hythe stood Saltwood Heights Battery, boasting four cannon, together with barracks for two thousand men. Along the coast, the harbour of Folkestone was protected by batteries on East Wear Bay and Bayle Fort. The latter

Sandgate Castle. Built on the orders of Henry VIII, this is how the castle looked in the mid-18th century.

ANNO TRICESIMO QUARTO

Georgii III. Regis.

C A P. LXXVI.

An Act for vesting certain Messuages, Lands, Tenements, and Hereditaments, in Trustees; for the
better securing His Majesty's Batteries, and other
Works, in the Counties of *Kent* and *Devon.*

[11th *June* 1794.]

WHEREAS, for better protecting such Part of the
Coasts of *Kent* and *Devon,* as lie open and exposed to
the Attacks and Depredations of His Majesty's Enemies,
it is highly expedient to strengthen and secure the Batteries and other Works erected on the said Coasts, and
in order thereunto, to purchase, among other Lands
and Hereditaments, the Lands herein-after mentioned, to be situate in
the Parishes of *Cheriton* in the said County of *Kent,* and *Brixham* in
the said County of *Devon :* And whereas divers small Dwelling Houses, situate on the East Side of *Warren Lane,* in the Parish of *Saint Mary
Warloiuk,* in the said County of *Kent,* lie so near to His Majesty's
Royal Laboratory in the Warren at *Weedenk* aforesaid, as, in case of
Accident by Fire, to endanger not only the said Laboratory, but also
His Majesty's other Buildings and Stores of War in the said Warren;
whereupon it is expedient to purchase the said Dwelling Houses for the
Use of His Majesty's said Warren : And whereas the said Lands situate

Act of Parliament 1794. This Act authorised the
purchase of land in Kent and Devon for use in
the defence of the country against invasion by
France.

had existed since at least the seventeenth
century, although its ordnance had been little
more than half a dozen 9-pounders. With the
heightened fears of invasion these were
upgraded to the much more effective 18-
pounders. Even the castle at Sandgate made its
contribution. Erosion by the sea meant that, by
1798, it was in *'a ruinous condition except the exterior
battery'.* Deemed not worth repairing, it was
nevertheless pressed into service, being
equipped with four 24-pounders in 1801.
However, the pride of place was held by
Shorncliffe Battery. In 1794 an Act of
Parliament authorised the purchase of 229 acres
of land just outside Folkestone for the purpose
of *"vesting certain Messuages, Lands, Tenements, and
Hereditaments, in Trustees for the better securing His
Majesty's Batteries and other Works".* The preamble to
the Act did not mention France by name but as
follows, *"for better protecting such parts of the coasts of
Kent...., as lie open to the Attacks and Depredations of His
Majesty's Enemies".* The land to be purchased was described as *"all that the said Piece or
Pasture Land called Shorn Cliff, belonging to the said James Drake Brockman (on Part whereof a Battery,
called Shorn Cliff Battery, hath lately been erected and built)"*. Situated between Seabrook and
Sandgate where the land rises steeply from the seashore to the hills behind, and with
its commanding presence over Hythe Bay, which was seen as the most likely landing
place for the invaders, there were twelve 24-pounders installed here in 1801.

The task of manning the batteries was divided between the Army and the Royal
Navy. Inland batteries, such as those at Saltwood Heights were tended by the Royal
Artillery, but the coastal forts, including Shorncliffe Battery, were the responsibility
of the Navy's Sea Fencibles. Supervised by regular officers, the Sea Fencibles were
also volunteers, predominantly fishermen, who agreed to serve one week in four.
They also maintained offshore armed patrols in Navy cutters.

The final element of home defence rested with the Regular Army. Although
these soldiers would have fared better in a fight than their comrades in the
Volunteers and Militias, there simply were not enough of them. Many had been
lost in the futile campaigns in Europe as part of the Duke of York's Expeditionary
Force, and many more were permanently stationed in Ireland, where the dual
threat of internal uprising and invasion by France were ever present. Such regular
troops as were stationed on the mainland were concentrated in strategically
located camps, ready to rush to vulnerable spots. In Kent, these camps were at
Chatham, Barham Downs near Canterbury, and Brabourne Lees near Ashford.

There was also a camp just outside Folkestone; its name was Shorncliffe.

Exactly when Shorncliffe had first been used for military purposes is not known. From its unique position, overlooking the Channel and with natural defensive qualities, it is likely to have been a favoured spot since time immemorial. There is reference in Leland to the finding of Roman coin near the site, suggesting that Caesar and his legions may have camped there. The first reliable reference is to be found in the "The British Army" by Sir

Shorncliffe Battery. A listed historical monument, the Battery Wall as it is today.

S.D.Scott who refers to the preparations to meet the Spanish invasion in 1588: *"The Charge of placing the coast of Sussex and Kent in the best state of defence was entrusted to Sir Thomas Scott and Sir James Hales. The former officer stationed two hundred and fifty men at Canterbury, from whence parties might be detached to oppose the enemy on the landing, and took up his station at Shorncliffe; while the other with the horse ranged the Downs."* Sir Thomas, in a letter that has the same ring of confidence as shown by another great commander of Shorncliffe over 200 years later, confidently predicted, *"I, at Shorncliffe, which I confidently holde, we may doe the best service that we shall be able to do, either by keeping the enemy from landing by decidering or diminishing some pts. Of his force, or at least by staying of him for a tyme."* We know that Queen Elizabeth stayed overnight at Sandgate Castle in 1588, and it is likely that she took the opportunity to speak to Sir Thomas and, perhaps, inspect the nearby camp.

With the outbreak of the Revolutionary Wars with France in 1793 activity at Shorncliffe camp resumed in earnest. In Stock's "Handbook of Folkestone" dated 1794 the following entry seems to refer to Shorncliffe, *"In June this year a camp was formed, consisting of three Militia regiments, the West Lowland Fencibles and a park of Artillery."* Another, and somewhat amusing, account confirms the presence of militia at the camp in the

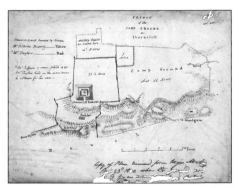

Shorncliffe Camp. This plan clearly shows the land occupied by the camp, including the Redoubt, the Battery and, between the two, the hospital. Although the date is unreadable, the absence of Martello Towers would place it between 1800-1805.

early 1790s. The Rutlandshire Regiment, the Old Buffs and the Berkshire Militia were at Shorncliffe when one of the Berkshire soldiers was discovered to be a woman (there is no mention of how the discovery took place). It is recorded that, *"her behaviour was so prudent in the regiment that the officers subscribed something handsome to clothe her properly and carry her home."* She had apparently served six years in the regiment without discovery. The Kentish Gazette reported that, in September 1798, the Prince of Wales visited the area to inspect the military stations at Hythe and

Shorncliffe, where he received a 20-gun salute.

The location of Shorncliffe camp on its high plateau, just a stone's throw from the water's edge, afforded commanding views across the English Channel and, on a clear day, to the French coast. In 1800 the camp included the recently constructed battery, referred to in the Act of 1794, and the barracks which, at that time, were a modest affair consisting of two L-shaped buildings turned towards each other so as to form a rectangle and surrounded by an earthwork redoubt. When serving at Shorncliffe the soldiers of George III would have to live in tents, pleasant enough during the summer months but, with its exposed location, uncomfortable during the winter. To the north of the camp was the village of Cherrington (as it was then called) and to the south, between the camp and the sea, was the village of Sandgate. Three miles to the west was Hythe which, although no longer enjoying the influence that its status as a Cinque Port had once afforded, was quite fashionable, and had a reputation as a pleasant watering place. Folkestone lay to the east but, in the early nineteenth century, it certainly could not claim to be fashionable, as graphically described in The Imperial Gazetteer,

> This town was one of the most disagreeable in England…and it presented every kind of repulsion to the visit of strangers. Its thoroughfares were ill paved and muddy; its streets were mere alleys, on steep inclines, partly progressing and partly communicating with one another by coarse flights of steps; and many of its houses were badly built, almost overtopped others, and contained hiding-holes and remote rooms for the storage of smuggled goods.

The village of Sandgate was no stranger to the martial ethos; during the eighteenth century England needed to maintain its naval supremacy during conflicts with France, Spain and Holland whilst, across the Atlantic, the colonists were struggling for independence from the mother country. Despite a population of just a few hundred Sandgate made a significant contribution to the fleet; no less than ten warships were built and launched from its shingle beach during the 1780s. There were three separate shipbuilding concerns clustered around Sandgate Castle. One of these, Fabian Clayton Wilson, built cottages for his workers and a surviving pair of these weatherboard homes can still be seen at the foot of Sandgate Hill. Amongst the ships built were the Dido, the Hussar and the Circe, all 28-gun 6th Rates, launched in 1784 and weighing nearly 600 tonnes apiece[1]. Other than shipbuilding, the local economy relied upon a brisk smuggling trade, as did much of the south coast. Shipbuilding came to an end with the outbreak of war with France, so the arrival of troops at Shorncliffe provided a welcome supplement to local trade.

The folk of Sandgate were, however, wary of anyone in uniform and had a

[1] See Appendix A for a list of ships built at Sandgate.

healthy disregard for authority. In 1801 the village hid three Frenchmen from English soldiers. Off the Sandgate coast a fierce battle had been taking place between two privateers, one French and the other English. For several hours they had been trying to outmanoeuvre each other until they came alongside, became locked together, and ran aground. There then followed terrible slaughter, but neither crew would concede to the other. At last, both sides being reduced to about a dozen men apiece, the English made a determined rush, killing all but three of the Frenchmen. The three survivors plunged into the sea and were rescued by

Folkestone. Smuggling and fishing were the staple trades of the town in the early 19th century.

the crowds who had gathered to watch the conflict. These three, it is said, were hidden by villagers from the English soldiers and eventually went on to marry local girls.

Facilities in Sandgate towards the end of the eighteenth century were modest, with the locals having for many years been served with just one public house. Established in 1736, the ambience of the Fleur de Lis can perhaps be judged from one 19th century description,

The Fleur de Lis. The first pub in Sandgate and a favourite haunt of smugglers. Vestiges of the building can be seen today.

(it) must have been chosen as a compliment to customers from the other side of the Channel. The very look of it is suggestive of smuggling forays and contraband trading; and if the old walls could speak no doubt they could tell many a stirring tale.

By 1798 the Fleur de Lis had been joined by the Trotting Horse and the New Inn, but the sleepy existence which Sandgate had enjoyed was about to change as the number of troops stationed at Shorncliffe camp was set to explode. For some years militia regiments had come to the camp for their annual training, joined by small detachments of the regular army, but it was much less important than Canterbury or Chatham, and was certainly not in the same league as Aldershot. Then, in 1802, Major-General John Moore arrived and under his command, Shorncliffe became a centre of excellence within the British Army, a position which it has ever since retained. In parallel with this development Sandgate rose to meet the demands of the influx of troops and visitors. The number of licensed premises increased, with the Military Tavern, Good Intent and Castle Inn serving one end of the market, whilst the Marine Hotel and the Duke of York satisfied those with finer tastes. At its peak, Sandgate could offer the thirsty visitor a choice of thirteen inns, hotels or public houses. There was a rash of house building to accommodate the officers and other visitors; the sleepy eighteenth century village was stirring and found itself popular and fashionable.

John Moore was the youngest of five children, and was born on the 30th November 1761, in the family home in the centre of Glasgow. Until he was thirteen the young Moore attended school in the city and had become, *'a boy of fiery and intractable temperament'*. Then, in 1774, his father, a physician and author, accepted a commission to take the sixteen year-old son of the Duke of Hamilton on an educational grand tour of Europe. He decided to take his son with them. In a letter home to his wife, Dr Moore describes their son, *'Jack is a really pretty youth; his face is of a manly beauty, his person is strong, and his figure is very elegant; he dances, fences and rides with uncommon address; his mind begins to expand, and he shows a great deal of vivacity tempered with good sense and benevolence; he is of a daring and intrepid temper, and of an obliging disposition. He draws tolerably; he speaks, reads and writes French admirably well...He is often operating in the field, and informs me how he would attack Geneva, and shows me the weak parts of the fortification...'*. It came as no surprise when the boy announced his wish to enter the army and, at the age of 15, he became an ensign in the 51st Regiment. With the outbreak of war with France in 1793 Moore saw action on several fronts, notably Corsica, St Lucia in the West Indies and Egypt. He gained a reputation as an innovative officer who cared for his troops and, when there was fighting, he led from the front. In November 1801 he arrived in Britain on board the brig Morgiana following the campaign in Egypt. The Peace of Amiens was signed in 1802 representing a brief respite in the struggle with

Major-General John Moore. In 1802 Moore began to train his Light Infantry Brigade at Shorncliffe.

Napoleon. Moore had been injured in Egypt, taking a musket ball in the thigh, so a period of recuperation was necessary. There were also family affairs to attend to following the death of his father in February 1802, but he soon found himself kicking his heels and was constantly harrying the War Department for an assignment. Despite his steady rise in rank, Moore had kept many of his youthful qualities, and his unrestrained honesty had not always sat well with his political masters. Nevertheless, his persistence was rewarded with the appointment, in September 1802, to the command of the Kent District.

Moore's district headquarters were at Canterbury but, in addition to his duties there, he was given approval to raise a new brigade. This brigade was to be unlike any other in the British army. It was to become the most highly trained and respected of British land forces and, eventually, was to play a major part in the final crushing of Napoleon Bonaparte; unfortunately General Moore would not live to join his men on the fields of Waterloo. The new brigade was called the Light Infantry, and Shorncliffe camp was to be its home.

After eight years of war with France the Peace of Amiens was agreed in October 1801, with the formal document being signed the following March. This Treaty created a long desired sense of peace for the country at large. In the euphoria that followed, the government, which was resistant to a large standing army, historically seen as a potential threat to parliamentary democracy, wasted no time in slashing the number of soldiers. This was a popular move in the country which had been suffering under high taxation to pay for the war. Even had the government wished to maintain or strengthen the army it would have had difficulty. Military service was generally unpopular; with a vicious disciplinary regime and pay inferior to that of the average agricultural worker, it tended to attract the dubious characters of society. Many recruits were either impecunious or seeking to evade the clutches of the criminal law. It was not unusual for a man condemned to death, or sentenced to transportation, to be offered the option of enlisting in the army, and it was an indication of the fate that awaited the recruit that many passed up the opportunity. Not only was the regular army decimated, but the half-million strong Volunteer army was also completely disbanded. It was in this difficult climate that John Moore arrived at Shorncliffe with plans to raise an elite brigade of soldiers.

Peace Medal. In anticipation of the Peace of Amiens, this medal was struck in 1802. The country was desperate for a halt in the war with France.

Ever since the wars in America during the latter part of the 18th century, the British army had employed light companies as elements within the traditional close ranked regiments. Acting as skirmishers they were given autonomy of movement, and would often engage the enemy before the massed ranks. General Moore, however, had much more visionary ideas for the light troops; rather than just companies of light soldiers he wanted entire regiments trained as light infantry. He was well aware of the state of the army and the quality of the average recruit; what he was looking for was a special breed of soldier. In January 1803 he wrote to Major-General Brownrigg, the Military Secretary, saying,

> The service of light infantry does not so much require men of stature as it requires them to be intelligent, hardy and active; and they should in the first instance be young, or they will neither take to the service nor be easily instructed in it.

Private of the 52nd Regiment of Foot. His redcoat made him more conspicuous in battle that the green-clad Riflemen of the 95th. The towns of south Kent teemed with thousands of his comrades during the Napoleonic Wars.

Moore was appointed Colonel of the 52nd Regiment of Foot and was given permission to train the regiment as a light corps. His first task was to recruit the right officers. This could be a delicate matter as seen from the tone of his letter to Brownrigg,

A most essential point is the choice of an officer to place at the head of such a corps, and fortunately the situation of the present lieutenant-colonels of the 52nd Regiment enables H.R.H. to remove one, or both of them, without injuring either their interests or their feelings, and of bringing forward officers who, with the necessary talents, have the inclination to dedicate their whole time to their duty. Of this description, Lieutenant-Colonel M'Kenzie of the 44th is one; and if H.R.H. chooses I can write to him on the subject.

As well as the 52nd, the Light Infantry was made up of the 4th, 59th and the 70th Regiments. The 43rd was also incorporated into the Brigade, some six months after the 52nd, but they did not arrive at Shorncliffe until June 1804. The final constituent of the new brigade was the 95th. Raised in 1800 as the Experimental Corps of Riflemen by Colonel Coote Manningham, another officer with vision, the 95th was brigaded in 1802. Men were chosen to join the Rifles. Each of 13 regiments was required to provide 33 soldiers, from officers to privates. They wore green jackets and pantaloons and were armed with the newly invented Baker rifle. General Moore must have been delighted to have the 95th join his Brigade and, on the 2nd October 1802, he wrote enthusiastically to Lieutenant-Colonel William Stewart, second in command of the 95th, suggesting a route for the march for the regiment to Shorncliffe from Ashford, and added, *"I hope you will find the station at Shorncliffe adapted to both your target practice and field movements."* One of the men who marched with the 95th to Shorncliffe was Rifleman William Surtees. Following transfers from the Northumberland Militia into the 56th Regiment, he had joined the Rifles in 1801, winning his corporal's stripes in October 1802. Surtees and his fellow riflemen were justly proud of their skill, although his description of Major Wade and Rifleman Seaton each holding the target, whilst the other shot at it from a distance of 150 yards, would be unlikely to find its way into modern training manuals.

Perched on high but level ground, and backed by downland on which the trees were mostly well-established beech and oak, Shorncliffe was ideal for training. A plan of 1801 shows the camp as consisting of some sixty acres, with about one third of this area consisting of wooded slopes, the remainder being relatively flat. The only buildings, apart from those associated with the battery, were the barracks, these being surrounded by a modest earthwork redoubt. This original redoubt was enlarged during Moore's command to enable his men to practice attacking and defending such a feature.

Acting independently, usually in pairs, the green-jacketed riflemen would move into tactical positions and armed with their new rifles, they would practice at picking off opposing troops, especially their officers. The other Light Infantry regiments, still armed with their Brown Bess smooth-bore muskets, specialised in speed of movement. Light troops were expected to think for themselves and to show initiative. In place of the 'flog and hang' system of discipline, Moore encouraged self-respect and self-discipline among his men. Another major innovation was the introduction of a new system of drill, replacing the stiff marching style of the Prussians, with the more natural gait which the British Army still uses today. Moore established a complete system of training, and this was put into effect by his Lieutenant-Colonels, notably MacKenzie and Stewart. Medals were awarded for good conduct and valour, a library was provided for the troops, and there were classifications for shooting and athletic prowess. The training of the Brigade required plenty of space and, early in 1803, General Moore urged that, if Shorncliffe was to be a permanent station, additional ground should be acquired. Large tracts of Government land, which had been let by the Ordnance Department to farmers, were reclaimed and a programme of land acquisition began. Although the ground at Shorncliffe was ideal for training, conditions initially were Spartan, with no barracks for the men whose only shelter was their tents. Even this was turned to an advantage as they were trained to prepare to strike camp and be ready to march out at an hour's notice. General Moore did, however, ensure that, during their first winter at Shorncliffe, most of his men were moved to permanent barracks at Hythe.

Shorncliffe soon echoed to the sounds of bugle and whistle. The drum, hitherto used as a means of issuing commands to regiments in the field, was unsuitable to fast moving troops over difficult terrain. The buglehorn, long used in fox hunting, was adopted and a system of signalling developed, with scores created for almost every conceivable military manoeuvre. General Moore

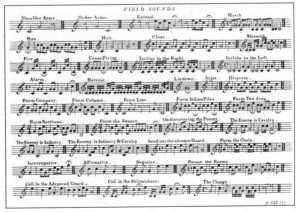

Sounds for the buglehorn. The Light Infantry was trained to respond to the sound of horn and whistle rather than the drum.

himself may have taken a key role in the decision to incorporate the bugle into the regimental uniforms of the Light Infantry; on the 30th January 1803, he recommended that the clothing of the 52nd should include,

> Wings to the men's Jackets — and to their Cap a green tuft — and instead of the Brass in front, a Bugle and Crown, or a Bugle only.
>
> To the Officers — jackets with two small Epaulets, with a Bugle on the strap. Caps such as the men's, and a short sabre.

Light Infantry shako. Displaying the buglehorn plate, the shako replaced the flatter headgear of the 18th century. As well as creating a more impressive sight to the enemy, the shako could be used as a pillow for the soldier at night and as a rest for his rifle.

The regiments of the Light Infantry and the 95th Rifles proudly incorporated the instrument into their shako plates, and the 'silver bugle' is still worn today by the successors of those early regiments, the Royal Green Jackets and the Light Infantry.

Whilst the rest of the country was revelling in the peace with France, the shaping of the Light Infantry Brigade continued throughout 1802. As the events the following year were to prove, the Peace was no more than an interlude, and the skills of the men trained at Shorncliffe would prove to be critical in winning the final victory over Napoleon. But that day was still a dozen years in the future.

Chapter 2

INVASION LOOMS

The French plans to invade England in 1798 had been interrupted by the Egyptian campaign, and General Bonaparte had been reassigned from the Army of England to supreme command of the Army of the East. By the time that campaign ended, Bonaparte had been elected First Consul and had taken to calling himself simply, 'Napoleon'. He lost no time in turning his attention back to the Channel coast. Whilst Britain had been troubled by the possibility of invasion during the closing years of the eighteenth century, the very real threat created during the years 1802 to 1805 was much more acute. Despite all of his conquests, Napoleon harboured one driving ambition; to invade Britain, this *perfidious Albion'*. It is impossible to calculate how much money he spent in seeking to fulfil his dream of marching through Kent, and planting his Imperial Eagles in London. At the height of the invasion threat, the country was in a state of terror at the prospect of falling under the sword of the French army. 'Boney' became the quintessential bogeyman, and naughty children of the time were told that he would come and eat them if they did not behave. A contemporary lullaby was obviously composed for the benefit of the wayward child,

French Invasion Map. This extract from a late 18th century French map shows the Channel, described by Napoleon as a 'ditch', which he contemptuously promised to jump.

Baby, baby naughty baby,
Hush you squalling thing. I say;
Hush your squalling, or it may be
Bonaparte may pass this way.

Baby, baby, he's a giant,
Tall and black as Rouen steeple;
And he dines and sups, rely on 't,
Every day on naughty people.

The peaceful interlude created by the Peace of Amiens lasted a little over a year, being shattered in March 1803 through Napoleon's double-dealing. On the 8th March, King George III sent a message to Parliament that it was necessary to prepare the country for war with France. In response, Napoleon issued an order on the 2nd May, effective from 7pm that evening, that, *"Tonight not an Englishman shall be visible in the most obscure theatre or restaurant in Paris."* His order continued, *"All Englishmen from the ages of eighteen to sixty, or holding any commission from His Britannic Majesty, who are present in France, shall immediately be constituted Prisoners of War."*

When the Peace had been announced late in 1801, tourists had flocked across the Channel to enjoy the delights of post-revolutionary France. Every night at ten o'clock there was a grand firework display in Paris, whilst the fashions and balls were truly avant-garde, as seen from the following description: *'Towards the close of supper, doors had been flung open, disclosing a garden, lit by coloured lamps, where trees bent beneath the weight of crystallised cherries, peaches and apricots, above fountains of iced orangeade and liqueurs. The female guests who wandered in this paradise had been appropriately attired, with naked arm, bare bosom, sandaled foot, circling zone and curled tresses.'*[2] With the resumption of hostilities there was a mass exodus of British visitors, but many had left it too late, and were rounded up by Napoleon's efficient police; these unfortunate souls were to remain in captivity for the next eleven years.

On the 20th May 1803, the Kentish Gazette announced that the English Ambassador to Paris had landed at Dover and that England had declared war on France. Napoleon began amassing an army along the French channel ports and soon thousands of labourers were set to work dredging the harbours and rivers of northern France. Camped along 10 miles of coastline were 120,000 seasoned troops, together with cavalry and supporting artillery. His shipyards were busy building a flotilla of 2000 flat bottomed ships, which would carry this 'Army of England' across the sea to the Kent coast. At home, fear of an invasion was heightened by propagandist rumours that the French were planning to land troops by balloon or even through a tunnel under the Channel. The

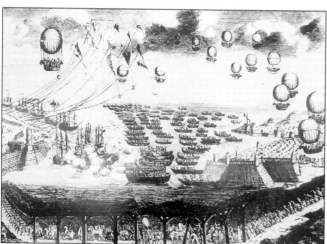

Invasion Routes. Propagandist cartoon suggesting the French might arrive by sea or air, or even by Channel Tunnel!

atmosphere reached fever pitch, and on church doors were pinned the rousing words of Shakespeare's Henry V from the Siege of Honfleur, *"Once more unto the breach..."*. Terrifying posters appeared depicting the horrors of invasion; mass rape of women and the slaughter of infants. On the other side of the Channel, the propaganda war was being fought with equal fervour. The newspaper, Le Moniteur,

[2] As described by Carola Oman in her book, *Napoleon at the Channel.*

reported that the inhabitants of Dover and Folkestone were already fleeing their homes at the sight of the bonfires of the invasion Army on the French cliffs.

With the country again in a state of war with France, General Moore was instructed to take immediate steps for the defence of the Kingdom. He was delighted to be given the honour of defending the Kent coast, on whose beaches the invasion force would land, and thus being set directly against Napoleon. Moore was a man of action and relished the idea of engaging the French, although he retained a professional respect for their leader. He wrote to one junior officer, who had gone to visit France during the Peace, "*I hope you will be introduced to Buonaparte. You will hear him plentifully abused here — but tho' he has done many acts which are unpardonable, yet I cannot help having admiration and respect for him.*"

Early in 1803, in his capacity as commander of the district, General Moore had set out to inspect the Kent coast fortifications. His conclusions made grim reading,

> From Deal to Dungeness is a long line. Dover and the castles of Sandown, Deal and Walmer may be susceptible of defence. The forts from Hythe to Dungeness are capable of none, but must be abandoned the moment a landing is effected. No infantry should be stationed in them, unless a few are necessary to assist the artillery in working the guns.

In early June of 1803, Moore had moved to Sandgate to prepare his brigade for war. The scheme of home defence at that time was based on the concept of "driving the country". In 1801 a comprehensive set of instructions[3] had been published by the Adjutant General for the information of the various Commanding Generals. Essentially, these involved retreating from the enemy once he succeeded in landing, and laying waste to land likely to fall into the enemy's hands, thus depriving him of the means of sustaining his army. The role of the army in Kent would be to harass the enemy and impede his advance on London until enough troops arrived for a counter strike. Moore did not agree with this strategy, as is clear from his letter to General Dundas, Commander of the South Eastern District:

> To Lieutenant General Sir David Dundas
> Sandgate, 1st July 1803
>
> Dear General,
> I am sorry to find from your letter that the former measures of driving the country are to be adopted....
> Most men, I take for granted, can fire and load a musket...
> The measures hitherto adopted have been with a view to drive and retreat, which leads to confusion and

[3] See Appendix B for full details of these instructions.

despondency, and is consistent with a warfare in which the French excel and to which the English are the least adapted. The language and system should be to head and oppose, and no foot of ground ceded that was not marked with the blood of the enemy. Nothing would dampen his spirits more than to see the country turn out against him. He knows the strength of our army – regular, militia and reserve – and will come prepared to meet, and may hope to beat it. But how penetrate or subdue a country where the population are armed and opposed to him? If the inhabitants of this neighbourhood occupied the heights, I should not doubt but that the force I have, thus aided, would drive into the sea any force France could send against us.

On the subject of coastal defences, Moore remained concerned and expressed this to Dundas,

Since I wrote last I have been with Colonel Twiss round Dungeness. The works at that place are so faulty, that it is hardly possible immediately to adopt measures to make them defensible. A tower in each of the five works would be requisite – and these would not be sufficient for the extent to be defended. It would be unwise to abandon this post. Colonel Twiss intends therefore to repair the stockading in the four forts and the centre redoubt, to mount four guns in the latter…Dungeness must be considered as a post of observation, and to give protection to ships anchoring…to oppose by its fire the disembarkation of troops; the moment the enemy are landed the garrison to retire, spiking the guns, and blowing up the ammunition….

General Moore's reference to towers was by no means a novel idea. Coastal towers had for centuries been placed around the Mediterranean as armed watchtowers. In 1798, a Captain Reynolds had advocated a line of English coastal towers on the basis that, *"There are no Works that appear to me so likely (to prevent an enemy landing) as a Simple Tower of Brickwork defended by a Handful of resolute Men."*

Moore himself was no stranger to the efficacy of the fortified coastal tower. In February 1794 the British fleet was sent to Corsica, the birthplace of Napoleon, to capture that island from the French. The initial seaward assault by warships of the British fleet was repulsed by a tower at Mortella Point. The army was then called in to make a landing and to attack the tower from landward and it was Lieutenant General David Dundas and Colonel John Moore who orchestrated that attack. From the following entry in Moore's diary, it is clear that he was impressed by the ability of the tower and its modest garrison to defend itself and the approaches:

Tower of Mortella, Corsica. The south coast Martello Towers were inspired by the ability of this small tower and its handful of men to repel the ships of the Royal Navy in 1794.

> When upon the heights reconnoitring, the day before, we saw the tower of Martello, behind which we had disembarked, and where the ships of war and transports still lay, attacked by the Fortitude, a 74, and Juno, 32-gun frigate. The tower had only two guns, but these were perfectly covered. The walls were 18 feet thick, of old masonry. An 18-pounder carronade was also mounted against it upon the land side at a distance of 200 yards. The ships were obliged in the course of the day to sheer off. The Fortitude lost above sixty men killed or wounded and Juno was set on fire and much disabled. In the course of next day more guns, which kept up a constant fire, were mounted on the land side; but such was the thickness of the walls of the tower that a breach was not effected. The officer, however, who commanded the tower, seeing the inutility of further resistance, since he had not been able to fire a single gun against the land battery, at length surrendered. He was a Garde Marine, and had eight or ten Grenadiers and some seamen with him two of whom had been severely wounded.

With Napoleon beginning to build up his forces on the other side of the Channel in preparation for the invasion, the idea of coastal towers was resurrected and, in 1803, Captain William Ford, a Royal Engineer, set to work designing and planning the construction of a chain of such towers. Due to Moore's inadvertent corruption of the name of the place in Corsica, Mortella Point, the towers became known as Martello Towers. However, it would be another year before construction of the towers was given approval.

Sandgate Beach. General Moore's mother and sister would have enjoyed walking along the beach during their stay in Sandgate in 1803. Painted by Capt William Ford in c 1810 (WD)

The weather during the summer of 1803 was perfect and it is not surprising that, given the natural charms of Sandgate, General Moore should invite his mother and sister, Jane, to join him. In July, he found lodgings for them near the castle at York Cottage, a small house, faced with weatherboard, painted white and run by a kind Kentish landlady. No doubt the General's ladies were able to make full use of the facilities described in The Hythe and Sandgate Guide, *"a News Room, Library, Inns and all the requisites to constitute a reputed bathing place and fashionable resort."* Or they may have preferred simply to enjoy the endless days of an exceptionally fine summer. For company, especially for his sister, Moore was confident that this could be provided by his officers. In March, he had written to a visiting friend, who wished to bring his stepdaughters with him,

> If the Miss Ords do not think they can trust the camp for
> beaux, or if they have any in attendance whose curiosity to
> see soldiers they may chuse to indulge, assure them that
> whoever accompanies them shall be cordially received by
> everbody here…

To enjoy the elegance of local society, a three-mile carriage ride into the fashionable town of Hythe provided the possibility of dancing at the Assembly, or a game of *Vingt-un* or *Quadrille* or one of a host of other card games which were the vogue, played on a Friday evening at the new Guildhall. Before Napoleon turned his attention across the Channel, Hythe had developed a reputation as a small but charming seaside resort. Apart from the fashionable promenades, there were footways leading to Saltwood where, according to a local guide of the period,

> The walks of which give a most comprehensive view of the inland country, capacious sea, and the busy shore beneath.

For those preferring horseback,

> The rides of pleasure that are usually chosen by those fashionable inhabitants who know the neighbourhood are as follows: In the chilly seasons of spring and autumn they commonly prefer the sheltered lowland ways...between Hythe and Sandgate; in more congenial weather they prefer the uplands; and where the highways of the county do not afford a road through the downs, they are intersected with those of the landholders, which are commonly sufficiently spacious for any carriage, and are open to the public.

During the summer of 1803 General Moore had much to occupy him. Between visiting his mother and sister, recruiting officers and training his men, and with a weather eye on Napoleon's preparations for invasion, he had also to prepare for a visit on the 1st August by the Commander in Chief, the Duke of York, who was coming to review his brigade.

Sandgate Beach and Castle.
Another painting by Captain Ford, this time showing Sandgate castle and a bathing machine. c1810 (WD)

Conscious of the royal appetite, he sent an order to Messrs Young of Dover which included 3 Hams, 6 Tongues, anchovy paste and a selection of cheeses.

Despite the threat from across the Channel, and perhaps even because of it, Shorncliffe attracted a good many visitors that first year. For amusement most of the society visitors and officers from the camp would resort to Hythe, but tiny Sandgate also had its attractions. The Kentish Gazette in 1809 extolled its virtues thus,

> The seabathing here is of the greatest perfection, as the waters are pure...its cliffs of easy ascent commanding a beautiful view of the British Channel, the undulating line of the French coast in the distance...

Similarly, another contemporary writer said,

> The inhabitants have rendered the little bathing place in every
> respect worthy of public patronage and encouragement.

Gaol delivery of Private McGee. After his arrest for rape and robbery, McGee was kept under lock and key by George Boxer, the Folkestone gaoler.

The common soldier, however, would have been drawn to the more prosaic charms of Folkestone where there were plenty of public houses to choose from, catering for the men of the local fishing fleet, the smugglers and traders. There were the expected incidents of drunkenness and rowdiness and occasionally far worse. Private Edward McGee of the 43rd Regiment found himself in the dock on the 22nd May, 1806, following an incident the day before. McGee appeared before Folkestone's Justices charged with, *"Feloniously committing a rape on the body of Martha May a single woman and for feloniously stealing taking and conveying away from her person divers Goods and Chattels belonging to her that is to say one Shilling in silver one pair of shoes one pocket handkerchief and a pair of silk gloves with a pocket."* A deposition was taken from the unfortunate Miss May. She described how, at about four o'clock the previous afternoon, she had been stopped in a Folkestone lane by a soldier who, after engaging her in conversation, dragged her into a ditch, where he raped and robbed her. Later, she had gone up to Shorncliffe camp and identified her attacker and the handkerchief that he had taken. Sergeant Major Bernard Murphy of the 43rd testified that a corporal and two privates had been sent the previous day to pick up any soldiers found in the vicinity of Folkestone, and that McGee had been apprehended and brought to the Guardroom as a result. On being searched a handkerchief had been found in McGee's cap. Asked how he came by it, McGee simply said he had had it for some time. The final piece of evidence was from Margaret Allen. She was at home at Foord in Folkestone when a soldier came in offering to sell a pair of silk gloves that he said he had found. He demanded half a crown but she offered a shilling, which the soldier took. Mrs Allen identified the

The Evidence of Martha May. This is the record of the evidence given by McGee's victim. She has signed simply with a 'X'.

Hot reception for Boney. This somewhat gruesome 1803 cartoon shows what the French invaders could have expected.

prisoner in the dock as the soldier. Miss May confirmed that the gloves sold to Mrs Allen were those stolen. For his part, Private McGee gave the following explanation of the events: He had left Shorncliffe Barracks and *"went into the Town of Folkestone via Sandgate and the Turnpike Road. I went into the sign of the Three Mackrell and had a pint of beer, then went up the road towards Dover past the Mill and from thence to the Red Cow and had a pint of beer there. I then headed back towards the Barracks when I was met on the road by a Corporal and two Privates who took me into custody and carried me to the barracks."* There he was confronted by Miss May who accused him of the crimes but, he claimed, he had never seen her before. As for the handkerchief, he said he had owned this for some time and it had an old mark on it. McGee was committed to stand trial at the 1806 Summer Assizes in Maidstone and was kept in Folkestone gaol until then. On the 28th July 1806, McGee came up before the Lord Chief Baron. He was found guilty of rape and robbery and sentenced to death. However, before the judges left Maidstone, they granted the former soldier a reprieve; he would spend many years in prison but his life would be spared.

In the same year a rather curious incident occurred, involving another soldier from the 43rd. Private William Killpatrick was charged with murdering George Moss of Burmarsh. The jury at the General Sessions sitting at the recently opened Guildhall in Hythe found that the defendant, *"not having the fear of God before his eyes, but being moved and seduced by the instigation of the devil with a certain pistol loaded with ball did then and there give to the said George Moss a mortal wound by violently, feloniously voluntarily and of his malice aforethought firing the said pistol at him, the said George Moss, whereby the ball entered the back of him and passing through his body came out two inches below his collar bone . . . of which mortal wound the said George Moss then and there instantly died."*

The truth, however, became apparent at the trial at Maidstone Assizes. Moss was a deserter from the 1st Battalion of Guards and his true name was John Hyman. He had deserted after having robbed a sergeant from the Coldstream Guards of his pocket book. Captain J Ellors of the 43rd had sent Killpatrick and another private to arrest the suspect who was working as a labourer on a gun battery. Moss resisted arrest and Killpatrick showed him that he was armed with pistols, and threatened to use them if necessary. Hyman took to his heels and Killpatrick drew his weapon and shot him. The verdict was manslaughter and Killpatrick served two months imprisonment.

Even the prestigious 52nd Regiment was not immune to the occasional soldier falling foul of the law, as in the case of Private Francis Grimm. He was charged with stealing, *"Six shoes of the value of Ten shillings."* At his trial before Folkestone Quarter Session, Grimm gave his account of how he came by the shoes. He said that he was quartered at the Folkestone Arms Inn and explained, *"I went home and pulled off my accurtrements and went to the Privy where I saw three pair of shoes lying altogether on the seat which I took into my own room...I took one pair to the Jolly Sailor where I met John Baker. I asked him whether he knew where I could sell a pair of shoes...he went out with them and soon after brought me 3/-."* The hapless soldier repeated this transaction with the other two pairs of shoes over the next couple of days. Unsurprisingly, Private Grimm was found guilty.

Despite these incidents, the civilian population generally welcomed the presence of the army at Shorncliffe. The trade they brought would have been impossible to replace. The merchants of Sandgate, having seen the influx of troops in 1803, had been alarmed to learn that they were the Light Infantry and, as such, could be required to strike camp and move out at an hour's notice. It was only when Major-General Moore had installed his mother and sister in the village that summer that they felt reassured that such a disaster was not likely to occur.

As the French preparations for invasion continued across the Channel, Napoleon, somewhat to the irritation of his naval commanders, became involved in formulating detailed plans for his fleet. His interest was almost obsessive; during the summer of 1803 he prescribed everything from the armament and complement of the flotilla to the number of cooking pots to be stowed aboard. There were four different designs of craft, the largest being the pramme, which was over 100 feet long and 23 feet in the beam. The smallest was the *peniche*, which was just 60 feet long and with a beam of only 10 feet and capable, in theory, of carrying five crew and fifty-five soldiers who were expected to row themselves across the channel, before disembarking and fighting their way ashore. There were those who doubted Napoleon's ability to mount an invasion. After examining one of the flotilla barges that had slipped its moorings and been picked up by the Royal Navy, a British admiral dismissed the

John Bull attacks. John Bull makes another appearance. Having become impatient waiting for Napoleon to launch his invasion, Bull sets off across the Channel. The Royal Navy did make a number of assaults on the Boulogne flotilla, sometimes firing shot into the French camp. From an 1803 watercolour.

threat if to be launched using such *"contemptible and ridiculous craft."*

By the summer of 1803 the idea of 'driving the country' and in its wake flooding the Romney Marsh had been abandoned. Defence of the realm would depend on repulsing the enemy by force of arms. A new Volunteer Act was passed by Parliament and by that autumn 463,000 men had enrolled in the nation's volunteer units. Unfortunately, only a third of this number could be equipped with muskets. At Shorncliffe, General Moore now had nearly 4000 regular troops in training and he was outwardly confident of his brigade's abilities. During a visit by his friend Thomas Creevey, the diarist and M.P., who was well aware of the growing threat from across the Channel,

William Pitt the Younger. Shown here in a contemporary illustration, Pitt is seen in front of Walmer Castle dressed in the uniform of Colonel of the Cinque Ports Volunteers.

Moore was asked, *"Are the French coming?"* The General replied, *"The invasion would, I am confident, end in our glory and his disgrace."* But if they came, persisted Mr Creevey, how would they be met? Moore was in no doubt. His Brigade would deal with the French in the water and, if they did reach dry land he would rely, *"Upon the people of England."*

Similar confidence can be seen when, in October 1803, Moore spoke to William Pitt who, as Lord Warden of the Cinque Ports had raised three battalions of the Cinque Ports Volunteers totalling 3000 men. The 3rd (Rye and Hastings) Battalion, consisted of twelve companies, including the 9th (Lydd), the 10th (Romney), the 11th (Hythe) and the 12th based in Folkestone. Pitt was a regular visitor to Shorncliffe and, on one such visit, he reassured General Moore that," *On the first alarm I shall march to aid you, with my Cinque Ports regiments and you have never told me where you will place us."* Pointing, General Moore said, *"Do you see that nearby hill? You and yours shall be drawn up on it where you will make the most formidable appearance to the enemy while I, with the soldiers, shall be fighting on the beach."* Pitt was spending a good deal of his time training his Volunteers at Walmer Castle, and would only leave them to travel to London if the prevailing wind ensured that the French could not launch their fleet. In a speech at a Volunteer banquet he reflected his faith in his men when toasting: *"A speedy meeting with our enemy on our own shores."*

Winston Churchill, with perhaps a trace of wry admiration, described the spectacle of *"...an ex-Prime Minister. Riding his horse at the head of a motley company of yokels, drilling on the fields of the South Coast, while a bare twenty miles away across the Channel the Grand*

Army of Napoleon waited only for a fair wind and a clear passage."

Moore displayed equal public confidence in the Volunteers, who spent their Sundays training in musketry. On a visit by Mr Creevey, the General is said to have called over a group of nearby Volunteers, and said to them, *"If the French come, I shall go with my men down to the beach, and you, my lads, will stand ready, I know, to help us on the hills."* One replied in broad Kentish brogue, *"We'll stand by you, General, depend on it. And say the word and we'll go down to the beach with you."*

Privately, however, General Moore was not so confident in the readiness of his men. The main obstacle to progress seems still to have been his ability to recruit the right officers. In a letter dated the 4th September 1803 he wrote:

> I had hopes, from the pains I have taken, and the mode I directed to be followed in the instruction of the regiments in my brigade, to have made much progress, and if honoured with another visit by H.R.H. to have shown him something tolerably perfect, but except in the 52nd the progress has been trifling. The other commanding officers, though many of them good enough men, have not military heads, and seem incapable of acting from general instruction.

General Moore was popular with his men, both officers and the rank and file. Charles Napier recalled an incident when Moore was going from his quarters in Sandgate up to the camp at Shorncliffe for evening parade. This was a steep climb and Moore challenged the half dozen or so officers with him, *"Now for a race to the top of the hill."* The General came second. On another occasion, when Thomas Creevey had been paying a visit, Moore invited him to go up and visit the camp. During their climb from Sandgate, they met a number of soldiers going down the hill in search of off-duty recreation in the village and, to a man, they all stood to as stiff as ramrods. The General put the men at ease and had a courteous word for everyone. He was also ready to take up matters with the civilian authorities on behalf of his men, as one local publican discovered in August 1805. It was reported in the proceedings of Folkestone Quarter Sessions that Edward Hopper, the licensee of the Ship Inn in Sandgate, had been refusing to take in soldiers who were quartered there. The General complained to the Mayor of Folkestone, with the result that Hopper was warned that, if he persisted, his licence would be revoked.

The highlight of 1803 had been the visit by the Commander in Chief to Shorncliffe in August, but there were other grand occasions. One was enthusiastically reported in the Kentish Gazette:

> Shorne Cliff Camp, Oct 13. We all had a grand field day here yesterday, which attracted an immense concourse of

spectators from all the surrounding country. The ground was crowded with pedestrians and equestrians of fashion, among whom was an assemblage of most beautiful women. The regular regiments, consisting of the 4th, the 70th, 59th, 52nd, and the rifle corps, with a party of artillery and two field pieces, were drawn up in the rear of the encampment about ten o'clock. The battalions having been formed into close column, Major General Moore and Staff arrived on the ground;-The Major General having taken the command, the rifle corps was ordered to advance and skirmish in front, where the enemy were supposed to lie concealed in a valley. The field pieces advanced at the same time to support it, and a brisk fire was kept up for a considerable time. The columns then formed the line, and advanced until they arrived at an opposite hill, where the line halted. Here the 52nd, being a light infantry battalion, extended, together with the rifle corps, and kept up a brisk fire to cover the line, which was ordered to retire, having first formed into close

column again...Among the spectators were Major General Forbes and Staff and Mr. Pitt, for whose satisfaction and entertainment the field day was ordered. He expressed himself exceedingly pleased at the rapidity and precision with which the 52nd performed all the light infantry manoeuvres, particularly at their dexterity and alertness in passing obstacles which presented themselves on the march.

The day was uncommonly fine; and when we could

Riflemen. The man kneeling is from the 95th, his comrade being from the 60th.

see the rival hills of the enemy's coast with the naked eye, it contributed in no small degree to render this grand military scene not only pleasing, but sublime and highly interesting.

As autumn 1803 dawned, the expectation of an invasion increased. The Volunteers were under orders to march at an hour's notice. William Wordsworth sought to capture the mood of the nation,

Now is the time to prove your hardiment!
No parleying now! In Britain is one breath;
We are all with you now from shore to shore:
Ye men of Kent, 'tis victory or death!

Rifleman Surtees recalls the atmosphere at Shorncliffe Camp, which he says was termed the *"Vanguard of England"*,

Napoleon studies his enemy. Standing on the cliffs at Boulogne, with his pavilion in the background, Napoleon looks confidently towards the coast of Kent.

…it was here that the threatened invasion of this country by Bonaparte must most likely have taken place, it being immediately opposite the grand camp then forming at Boulogne. Daily rencontres took place between our cruisers and his far-famed flotilla; and on one occasion, the belief that he was sending forth his invincible host was so great that our camp was struck, the troops turned out, and each man received his sixty rounds of ammunition; the wagons and carts were all put in immediate requisition, and the inhabitants were flying in all directions. But to our disappointment, I will not say whether disagreeable or otherwise, it all ended in smoke; it happened to have been some of his flotilla making a movement along the coast, which had been set on by our cruisers and pretty roughly handled.

This may well have been the same false alarm that, in September 1803, found General Moore inspecting defences at Dungeness, when a jumpy duty officer at Folkestone signalling station had misread a message, and thought that the enemy fleet had put out of Calais. Moore rode back to Shorncliffe, recalling,

My horse suffered; I galloped him the

John Bull stands firm. As if he is staring back at Napoleon, John Bull shows the right combination of resolution and contempt. From an 1803 watercolour.

whole way back. The Volunteers, Sea Fencibles and all were turned out, and very cheerful – not at all dismayed at the prospect of meeting the French; as for the Brigade, they were in high spirits. By the time I reached camp the mistake was discovered.

Despite the Channel winds blowing in Napoleon's favour that autumn, his invasion fleets never left their harbours. His plans were beset with problems; hopeless delays in the shipyards and money running short. The harbour facilities were found to be so inadequate that it would take several days to launch all of his barges. Undaunted, on a visit to Boulogne on the 16th November, he sent a message to Paris,

> From the cliffs of Ambleteuse I have seen the English coast
> as clearly as one sees the Calvary from the Tuileries. You
> can make out houses and movement. It is a ditch which
> will be leaped whenever one has the boldness to try.

Meanwhile the warships of the Royal Navy prowled the Channel, ready to pounce on any vessel unwise enough to leave the safety of her moorings. The First Lord of the Admiralty, Lord St. Vincent, whose ships were everywhere blockading the French Grand Fleet spoke with supreme, yet justified, confidence when he predicted, *"I do not say the French cannot come, I only say that they cannot come by water!"*

With the onset of winter and the threat of invasion over for that year, and whilst his brigade moved into winter quarters, General Moore had found himself accommodation in Sandgate. He sat down in a rare spare moment to write to his mother, who had moved back to the family home at Marshgate near Richmond,

> Sandgate
> Thursday night 1803
>
> My dear Mother,
> I despair of an opportunity of writing to you in the
> forenoon, so I shall seize one before I go to bed, where it is
> not very likely that I shall be interrupted. The breaking up
> of the camp and the settling of the troops in their quarters
> is one more additional employment. We had three or four
> clear frosty days to do it in and they are all now snug, not
> in the best barracks but in such as appear to them
> comfortable, after the wet and bleak tents on Shornecliff.
> I have got Sir John Shaw's house for three guineas a week
> during the winter months; in summer it will of course be
> at least double. Every soul has left. In Shornecliff Barrack

which is the only one nearer to me than Hythe there is but a small regiment. I have no prospect of society. I have therefore sent for my books. My mornings will be occupied as usual, but in the long evenings the books will be my sole resource. I consider invasion over for this winter, and therefore probably over for ever, but with the winds I now witness a naval expedition cannot be undertaken; therefore send me your recipe for minced pies, yours to my taste are the best I meet with. Kind remembrance to Jane – good night, my dear Mother.

Believe me,

Ever affectionately, John Moore

As he returned to his Sandgate lodgings, having ridden down from the camp on wet and windy winter nights, General Moore would cast his eye across to 'the Iron Coast', and be able to retire in the knowledge that the country was secure for another night. When he was not entertaining, Moore passed his evenings reading his books which had been sent down from London. Most of his collection had a military bias; the works of Sontag, de Rottenburgh and Tielke, but pride of place was taken by Julius Ceasar. Moore's only concession to light reading was the complete works of William Shakespeare and the poems (in Scottish) of Robert Burns. The General regularly welcomed junior officers to his home and, after browsing his collection with awe, they would leave somewhat daunted by their General's taste in literature, and the prospect that they would have to master such works if they had aspirations to emulate him.

The year 1804 arrived, but still Napoleon did not. Yet there was always the danger of the French advance guard of 4000 picked Grenadiers slipping past the British

Hythe Theatre. Advertising a production at Hythe's theatre in March 1809. It is not known whether the performers were officers and wives of the 95th Rifles or local thespians. The theatre has long gone, but Theatre Street remains as a reminder.

naval squadron in the fog and making a landing on the beach below Shorncliffe. General Moore had almost as many troops now stationed at Shorncliffe, trained and ready. As one commentator put it, if the French did attack, *"There would have been such a fight as has rarely been seen."*

The soldiers at Shorncliffe were supplemented by those stationed in Hythe. At the turn of the 19th century these troops were mostly from the county militias. From Baptism records for St. Leonards Church in 1799, the East Suffolk Militia and the Cheshire Militia seem to have had the greatest presence, but with a good showing also from the Fifeshire Fencibles. The Royal Artillery represented the regular army. After 1800 there was a steady increase in soldiers based in the town and, at the height of the Napoleonic wars Hythe was home to over ten thousand men which, for a civilian population of below two thousand, imposed considerable challenges upon local facilities. To house the men, weatherboard barracks were being built and soon they began to dominate the slopes at the western end of the town. These were still evident when William Cobbett travelled through Hythe on his Rural Rides in the 1820s, and they attracted his critical attention, *"half barracks; the hills are covered with barracks; and barracks most expensive, most squandering, fill up the side of the hill."*

Only a few of the rank and file soldiers of the early nineteenth century left accounts of their experiences, but one who did was Benjamin Harris. As he spent time in Hythe barracks and at Shorncliffe, his recollections give a rare glimpse into these early days. Harris was born in Wiltshire and helped his father to tend sheep on the downs of Blandford in Dorset until his name was drawn in a ballot and he joined the 66th Regiment of Foot. However, the minute he set eyes on the 95th Rifles, Harris was drawn by their smart, dashing and devil-may-care appearance and he managed to secure a transfer and marched with the regiment to Hythe.

Harris recounts the sad story of Sergeant Thomas Mayberry, who was a well-respected and honest soldier, until he stole two hundred pounds from the men in his company, money intended to pay for provisions supplied to the men. He lost the money in what Harris called, *"the society of gamblers, who at that time infested the town of Hythe."* It was certainly true that Hythe had its fair share of rogues and, in common with Folkestone and Sandgate, attracted the smugglers, but perhaps Harris is painting an unduly bleak picture of the town that also had its respectable inns, assembly rooms and also a theatre built especially for the troops. However, the result of Sergeant Mayberry falling into the company of Hythe's ne'er-do-wells was that a number of local traders remained unpaid. Mayberry was brought before a court martial where he was convicted and sentenced to receive seven hundred lashes. On the day of punishment the regiment, as was the tradition, was formed into a square at Hythe barracks to witness the event. Also there was a man named Gilbert, who was one of the traders who had been defrauded, and who had apparently expressed to some of Mayberry's companions that he was content to lose the money provided, *"he saw the fellow flogged."* Mayberry was marched into the square, tied to the punishment triangle and received his seven hundred strokes without a

Recruiting Party in Sandgate. Redcoats trying to entice locals to accept the King's shilling outside the New Inn. Painted by Captain William Ford c 1810. (WD)

murmur. Thereafter his fellow soldiers, officers and men alike, shunned him. But the opportunity came for Mayberry to redeem himself; he volunteered for service in Portugal and, at the siege of Badajoz, displayed such bravery that his captain commended him on the spot with the reassurance that *"you have this day done enough to obliterate your disgrace; and, if we live, I will endeavour to restore you to your former rank."* Mayberry was ordered to the rear but, despite already bearing several wounds, he refused, *"No going to the rear for me, I'll restore myself to my comrades' opinion, or make a finish of myself altogether."* Shortly after, whilst in the thick of the fighting, Mayberry's skull was split in two by the blow from a French sabre.

Rifleman Harris went to Spain with the 95th Rifles and took part in the heroic retreat to Corunna in 1809. On their return the 2nd Battalion, together with the 43rd and 52nd Regiments were paraded at Hythe, but the troops were in a sorry state. Having been disembarked at Dover, many died there with the remainder being expected to find their own way to the barracks. Harris recalled that when he *"sat down exhausted by the road-side several times during the march, and looked at the men, I thought it bore in some degree a similitude to the Corunna retreat, so awfully had disease enfeebled them."* At Hythe the hospital was filled to capacity with the sick and dying and for many their final resting place was a grave near to the hospital. Harris was one of the lucky ones to recover from the ordeal, and he was sent out recruiting to fill the depleted ranks of the 95th.

In the same way that he had been attracted to the uniform of the 95th, Harris found that, along the coast, militia troops were easily tempted to join the Rifles. The men of the East Kent Militia at Lydd were soon following Harris and his swaggering companion, Sergeant-Major Adams who *"had a sling belt to his sword like a field officer, a tremendous green feather in his cap, a flaring sash, his whistle and powder-flask displayed, an officer's pelisse over one shoulder, and a double allowance of ribbons in his cap."* At Hastings, the two men of the 95th had great success in persuading one hundred and twenty five men and two officers of the Leicester Militia, who had given their names to the 7th Fusiliers, to change their minds in favour of the Rifles.

Harris gives a poignant description of the recruiting process. After he and Sergeant-Major Adams paraded themselves in their uniforms they would treat potential recruits to 'entertainment' and plenty of alcohol. Many hapless souls 'volunteered' whilst under the influence of drink. The recruit would be given his ten guinea bounty, which most spent on drink and other excesses. Harris then describes what he calls 'the reaction', *"The drooping spirits, the grief at parting with old comrades, sweethearts, and wives, for the uncertain fate of the war. And then came on the jeers of the old soldier; the laughter of Adams and myself, and comrades, and our attempts to give a fillip to their spirits as we marched them off from the friends they were never to look upon again; and as we termed it, 'shove them on to glory' – a glory they were not long in achieving, as out of the hundred and fifty of the Leicestershire we enrolled…scarce one man…could have shown at the year's end some token of the field he had fought in; very many found a grave, and some returned to Hythe with the loss of their limbs."*

During the same period that Rifleman Harris was stationed at Hythe, a young man had joined the 52nd at Shorncliffe camp. John Dobbs had received his commission into the regiment in Dublin, and attributed this to the fact that his father had been a school friend of General Moore. His battalion was in training at Shorncliffe and Dobbs describes his time there,

> I found myself in the midst of perfect gentlemen. The duty was carried on like clockwork, and scarcely any wine drank at the mess, frequently none. After dinner we used to spend the evening playing foot-ball, rackets, &c.: we had constant roll-calls for eye washing; every man was paraded with the lid of his camp-kettle full of water which they washed them with. I was not allowed to take command of a section going to church till I finished my drill. In drill every man was taught his centre of gravity by the balance step, - to take an exact length of pace by the pace stick, - to step in slow, quick and double quick, by the plummet and tap of the drum, afterwards to move in bodies or extended order and out post duty, &c.
>
> The officers having to go through every part of it, the drill was brought to such perfection that a line of 1000 men has been known to march over Shorncliff without any perceptible departure from their dressing.

Whilst much of Dobbs' description can be understood by any modern-day soldier, his reference to the ritual of 'eye washing' is less familiar; it may have been deemed necessary to rid the eyes of the corrosive black powder from musket firing.

In 1804 a dramatic change in British domestic politics occurred, with William Pitt being re-installed as Prime Minister. Although Pitt was reluctant to oust the ineffectual Addington, the mood of the House of Commons and the country at large thrust him into the role that he had only vacated a few years before. In a speech to the House on the 25th April, it was clear that, for Pitt, there could never be any question of peace with Napoleon,

> I need not remind the House that we are come to a new era in the history of nations; that we are called to struggle for the destiny, not of this country alone, but of the civilised world...Amid the wreck and the misery of nations, it is our just exultation that we have continued superior to all that ambition or that despotism could effect; and our still higher exultation ought to be, that we provide not only for our own safety, but hold out a prospect to nations now bending under the iron yoke of tyranny of what the exertions of a free people can effect, and that, at least in this corner of the world, the name of liberty is still revered, cherished and sanctified.

It was one of those curious historical coincidences that saw Pitt resume the reins of power on the very day, the 19th May 1804, that Napoleon was declared Emperor of the French.

That summer witnessed Napoleon, perhaps in an attempt to draw attention away from lack of any invasion, staging a number of theatrical pageants in Boulogne. A pavilion was erected; the ceiling of its Chamber depicted an eagle flying through gilded clouds and discharging a thunderbolt against Britain. The Army of England, which had by now grown to an estimated 175,000 men, was camped along the coasts of northern France. The camps took on an air of permanence as wooden huts were erected around which the soldiers cultivated vegetables and flowers in neat little gardens. Thousands of vessels were moored at jetties and quays ready to take the invasion army and its ordnance across the Channel, escorted by a squadron of men-of-war. From Sandgate, where he was now residing, General Moore wrote to his mother, "The collection at Boulogne can only mean this part of the coast, and I am pleased with the prospect of seeing the first of it. If we beat the French handsomely in the first instance, the house at Marshgate will not hold you."

In June 1804 the 43rd Regiment of Foot arrived at Shorncliffe from the Channel Islands. Moore had served with them in St. Lucia and Egypt, but they had been through a bad time, with their depleted ranks having been supplemented by two

The Boulogne Camp. Napoleon is seen distributing the Legion d'Honneur to soldiers of the Army of England in August 1804.

regiments of disbanded fencibles. But it would not be long, under General Moore's guidance, before the 43rd would serve as equals alongside the redoubtable 52nd. Once again, the stage was set and the country braced for invasion. In the same month that the 43rd arrived to complete Moore's brigade at Shorncliffe, the following morale boosting verse appeared in the national newspapers,

> Let the tyrant of France still threaten our coast
> Of invincible standards they've told us before,
> We've courage and honour and valour to boast,
> And tho' they have thousands, we've Moore!

Across the Channel, Napoleon continued to posture. On the 20th July 1804, despite a strong gale and advice to cancel, a review of the invasion flotillas was held which resulted in several hundred of his men being drowned. Napoleon chose the day of St. Napoleon, the 15th August, as his official birthday, and the celebratory gunfire could clearly be heard at Shorncliffe. The following day he presented the *Legion d'Honneur*, the award he had introduced two years earlier, to the leaders of the Army of England. As if in reply, Shorncliffe echoed to cannon fire when, on the 23rd August, the Duke of York came to inspect the brigade. General Moore was pleased with the event and he wrote to his mother,

> My troubles are now over, and everything private as well
> as public passed off very well. Our review was at seven
> o'clock on Thursday morning. At first the day lowered,-

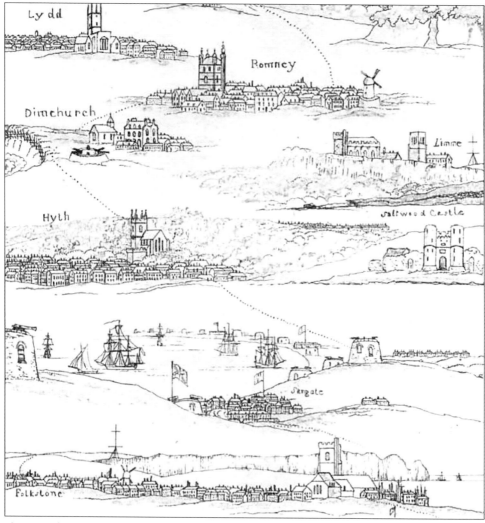

The Coast of Conflict. A novel map from the Hythe and Sandgate Guide of 1809, showing the defences along the south Kent coast.

rained a little and threatened more; but at last cleared up, and was very fine. I took advantage of some ground upon the right of the camp, in the direction of Cheriton Church which is woody and broken, and placed the troops upon it, so as to have a very good effect. We there fought a battle, the troops did their parts well. The style of the review was quite different from that which you saw; it was different and better than any the Duke had seen, and was much applauded, both by the ladies and the military connoisseurs: in short we came off with flying colours.

Notwithstanding all the honour, and all the flattering compliments, still the four days attendance completely wore me out. I rejoiced most heartily when they were over.

In contrast to the previous year, with the country as a whole much less preoccupied with invasion fever, the summer of 1804 did not attract the same interest from visitors and the season at Shorncliffe was quiet. But just because his men were not under public scrutiny did not mean that General Moore allowed them to relax. The Kentish Gazette reported on the 21st June,

> Shorn Cliffe Camp.
> The 43rd and 52nd regiments of foot have been reinforced within this day or two, by upwards of 400 men from the Army of Reserve, to complete the two regiments. The ground in the front of the camp is occupied from morning til night with the Regiments drilling. Orders have lately been issued by Gen. Moore, that the 95th or Rifle Corps, should be practiced in the mode of firing, from the edge of the cliff to a target placed on the Water's edge.

General Moore was wise not to relax in his training and preparations; Napoleon was planning a two-pronged attack during the autumn of 1804, as his orders to General Berthier reveal:

> September 27th, 1804.
> Cousin,
> The expedition to Ireland is settled. We have the means of embarking 18,000 men at Brest...The Grand Army at Boulogne will embark at the same time, and do everything that is possible to effect a landing in Kent.

Whether General Moore knew of Napoleon's plans at this time is not known, but it is likely that he did; there was a constant campaign of infiltration of the camp at Boulogne in efforts to obtain intelligence about French activities and intentions. This was a hazardous pursuit. In July 1804, eight well-dressed Englishmen were arrested near Boulogne harbour in possession of incendiary materials. They were shot within an hour. Another spy was caught on the cliffs waving his arms. It was alleged that he was signalling to British ships, he was court-martialled and shot the next day.

The main item of social news at Shorncliffe that year was that Colonel Kenneth MacKenzie of the 52nd, a popular officer and a favourite of Moore's, had fallen under the spell of Miss Rachel Andrews, the only daughter and heiress of Robert Andrews of Hythe. The year still had one surprise for General Moore. On the 28th

September he learned that he was to be knighted. In a letter to his mother, Moore's reaction was predictable: *"Sir John and a ribbon seem not in character with me."* After his investiture and return to Shorncliffe camp one of the General's aides-de-camp became carried away with too many 'Sir Johns' and was roundly rebuked. *"Sir! I am your General. I am General Moore."*

Chapter 3

MARTELLO TOWERS AND MILITARY CANAL

Since resuming his position as Prime Minister in May 1804, William Pitt had moved from Walmer Castle and returned to London. The Duke of York, as Commander-in-Chief, had approved Captain Ford's plans for the Martello towers the previous year but, since then, the subject had become embroiled in politics. Whilst Ford's plans had been gathering dust, another military engineer, Lieutenant Colonel John Brown, had been inspecting the south coast defences and, on the 19th September 1804, he presented his report to Sir David Dundas. Brown reached the same conclusions as General Moore had in 1803, *"The landing on this part of the coast is*

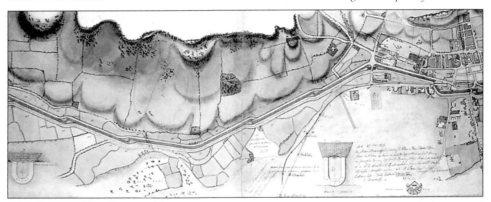

The Royal Military Canal, Hythe. The canal as it enters Hythe from the west. From the beautifully drawn Canal Book which is on display at Hythe Library and Museum. The whole length of the canal, together with other key military features, is contained in the book.

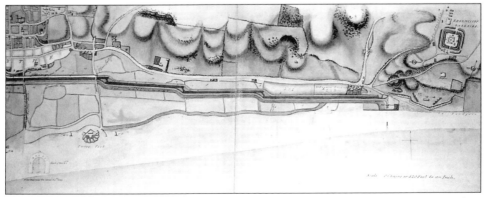

The Royal Military Canal, Shorncliffe. A continuation from the previous illustration, the canal here emerges from the east of Hythe and continues to its destination below Shorncliffe camp.

extensive. . .and. . .the present batteries are placed at a considerable distance from each other and could make little or no resistance after the enemy had gained the beach." Colonel Brown's solution was not to build towers but a canal, from Shorncliffe Battery to Pett in Sussex, a distance of nearly thirty miles.

John Brown was a Scotsman born in 1756. He served as a military engineer and surveyor in the West Indies and Ireland. In 1796, following the appearance of the French fleet at Bantry Bay, he was sent there to erect batteries, and from there, in 1797, to construct defences at Cork Harbour. Unfortunately, the defence works at Cork collapsed after heavy rain and Brown came in for some criticism. In January 1798, none other than John Moore, then a Colonel in the 51st regiment, had been appointed to command the fort at Cork harbour and, from his diary, we learn that *"I remained at Cove till the 22nd January, during which time I inspected minutely the state of the forts and defences of Cork harbour. In all wars it (Cork harbour) has been a point of jealousy, and large sums have been expended on its defence, but with so little judgment that it is still in a precarious state, and upon the whole the works at Cork harbour are a disgrace to the country."* Despite these criticisms, Brown's career seems not to have suffered and, in May 1802, he was appointed Lieutenant-Colonel Commandant of the Royal Staff Corps.

On the face of it, the country had a choice; Towers or Canal. Within days of receiving a copy of Brown's report in September, and despite having already signalled his approval to the system of towers, the Duke of York wrote to Lord Camden, the Secretary of War, *"In regard to the proposal of cutting a canal betwixt Hithe and the River Rother, for the purpose of military defence, by separating an enemy landed upon the coast of Romney Marsh from the interior of the country, I am to press this measure most earnestly upon the consideration of His Majesty's Government."*

It was never intended by either Captain Ford or Colonel Brown that the towers and the canal should go hand in hand: each was a separate entity which would be capable of defending the south coast. As events unfolded, however, both options were adopted, and William Pitt can be credited with much of the responsibility for this decision.

The canal project received almost immediate government approval, but there was considerable resistance by local landowners to part with the land necessary for its construction. With the French threat unabated, if the canal was going to be built before it was too late, these influential men had to be brought round quickly. On the 24th October 1804 a meeting was called at Dymchurch in Kent. Pitt attended and brought with him not only his authority as Prime Minister but also, and perhaps more significantly, that of Lord Warden of the Cinque Ports. With a *'perspicacity peculiar to himself'*, he was able to convince the majority of those present, not only of the pressing military need, but also of the benefit to them of the canal. Whether by accident or design, Pitt had been at a meeting the previous month, when he had delivered the bad news. The Kentish Gazette reported that:

On Thursday last Mr Pitt, accompanied by Generals Twiss

and Moore, met the Lords and Bailiffs of the Level of Romney marsh at new hall Near Dymchurch, to consider the best mode of inundating the marsh in case of invasion, when it was determined that, on the appearance of the enemy on the coast, the sluices should be opened, to admit the sea so as to fill the Dykes, which might be accomplished in one tide and in the case of actual invasion remain open another tide, which would be sufficient to inundate the whole level.

The flooding of the Romney Marsh was an unwholesome prospect for the landowners, as the sea water would render their land barren for years to come, so when Pitt came back to Dymchurch in October, he was able to deliver the good news. The canal would avoid the need for them to retreat from and flood their land and, as a bonus, it would improve both the drainage and irrigation of their land. Armed with the landowners' signatures, Pitt was able to order work to commence on

Construction of the Royal Military Canal. A modern artist's impression of the building of the canal. This, and other interpretations, can be seen at Martello Tower 3 on Folkestone's East Cliff.

what became the Royal Military Canal, and the first pick broke ground on the 30th October 1804.

As for the Martello Towers, the problem seemed to be inertia rather than opposition. Captain Ford's plans had been languishing before one committee or another for over a year. Earlier in the year one committee report had concluded that,

> Towers as sea batteries appear to have little or no advantage over any other battery of the same number of guns.

William Pitt was not so sure; he had inspected the coastline and personally selected a number of potential sites for towers. Three days before his meeting in Dymchurch to argue the case for the canal, he had gone to a meeting in Rochester which had been called by the Privy Council. The agenda was to consider the whole system of coastal defences and in attendance were many senior political and military figures, including Generals Twiss and Moore, both strong advocates of the towers. The only person to speak out against the towers was Lieutenant Colonel John

Seabrook Redoubt today. Built as an addition to Shorncliffe Battery wall, the redoubt continued the walled defences to the Canal. Cannon were placed within the redoubt.

Brown, the proponent of the canal, who roundly condemned the *"expensive and diabolical system of Tower Defence."* Despite Brown's opposition, the meeting concluded that the south coast towers should go ahead and that 81 of them should be built.

John Rennie, the builder of London and Waterloo bridges, was appointed as consulting engineer to the canal project, and he set about resolving a number of technical issues, such as depth, width, how to line the canal and how to prevent flooding during construction. Bridges had to be considered both from the point of view of cost and ease of removal in the event of invasion. Key features included a 'dog-leg' at regular intervals, enabling cannon to fire upon enemy troops trying to cross the canal. Even before they reached the canal, the French invaders would come under withering fire from British troops, stationed upon fire steps behind a protective earthwork parapet, on the landward side of the canal. The Shorncliffe Battery wall was to be extended to the eastern end of the canal where a redoubt would be formed. Together with a new military road running behind the canal, enabling troops and supplies to be rushed to any vulnerable point, the canal may well have proved a much greater obstacle to Napoleon's forces than some sceptics believed.

Similarly, the Martello Towers were the subject of several design alterations, one of the first blueprints having been for a rectangular design. A key issue was the ability of the towers to withstand cannon fire and, to determine the strongest bonding for the brickwork, experiments were carried out by the Royal Engineers at Woolwich. By a process of trial and error, where cannonballs were fired at different prototypes, the maximum strength was found in a mortar of lime, ash and hot tallow which, when set, was as hard as iron. The contract for the construction of the towers

Inside a Martello Tower. Showing the first floor accommodation for the garrison troops. The vaulted ceiling is necessary to provide the strength to hold the 24-pound cannon on the roof of the tower. Note the rack around the central pillar for muskets to be stored. (WD)

was awarded to William Hobson and he began with the three towers to the east of Folkestone in the spring of 1805. Even as they were being built, the design of the towers was being amended. Four Martellos were built along the seaward perimeter of Shorncliffe camp itself and, from his eyrie in Redoubt Barracks, John Moore was able to see the towers taking shape, especially in the evenings when their dark shapes were etched against the Channel skies.

Below Shorncliffe the much-neglected Sandgate Castle, designed to repel the French and Spanish nearly three hundred years earlier, was given a new lease of life by conversion to a 'Super-Martello'. The three bastions were reduced in height and strengthened with an additional thickness of brickwork, and the central keep was reinforced and given the distinctive vaulted roof strong enough to hold the traversing cannon on the gun platform above. The towers would be spaced at 600 yard intervals, so that the 24-pound cannons could provide overlapping arcs of fire. It was calculated that any enemy warship coming within range could be simultaneously bombarded by the cannons from no less than fifteen towers. The Martellos were to be garrisoned by one officer and 24 men with their accommodation on the middle floor and stores, including powder and shot, being stored on the floor below.

Tower 24 today. Martello Tower 24 at Dymchurch clearly shows the 24-pound cannon and the traversing mechanism enabling a 360 degree arc of fire.

Early in 1805, having crowned himself King of Italy, Napoleon sent totally unacceptable peace proposals to his 'brother', King George III. As spring passed into summer, it seemed that Pitt's hope to form a powerful land force on the continent by means of a coalition with Austria, Sweden and Prussia and, most importantly, Russia, would be fulfilled. Whilst Britain still dominated the seas, there could be no victory on land without such an alliance. Meanwhile the continued threat of invasion lurked across the Channel. But Napoleon's obstacle remained the Royal Navy. He devised a plan, detailed in his Grand Design issued on the 22nd March 1805, to despatch his fleet to the West Indies and thereby to lure the British fleet into giving chase. Then, eluding the British in the Caribbean, his ships were to double back with all speed, to arrive in the Channel in July with the Combined Fleet of 60 battleships. Napoleon would then be free to launch his invasion flotilla, free from molestation by the Royal Navy. All he required was *"A favourable wind, and thirty six hours."* Napoleon's plan only partially succeeded; Nelson and much of the fleet was drawn off to hunt down Admiral Villeneuve and the French navy, but the British admiral gave orders for the Channel Fleet to be reinforced as a precaution.

General Moore returned to Shorncliffe early in 1805, following a covert mission to Ferrol in Spain. In his absence Kenneth MacKenzie had married Rachel Andrews. The wedding had taken place at Canterbury on the afternoon of the 16th December. Moore had hoped to be back in Sandgate in time for the ceremony but was still on board HMS Indefatigable off the coast of Spain. On arrival back at Shorncliffe, he found that the ranks of his Light Infantry Brigade had been supplemented by drafts from various militias. Moore was delighted to welcome to the ranks of the 52nd a contingent from the Renfrew Militia. He thought highly of Scotsmen and would have liked to recruit more, *"I am partial to them as soldiers, and in general they are better educated, and consequently become better and more useful non-commissioned officers than either the English or the Irish."*

Again the country was gripped with fear of invasion. Napoleon had visited Boulogne on a number of flying visits and as the increased activity through his presence was spied through the English telescopes, so the anticipation of an attack increased. The troops at Shorncliffe took to practising repelling invaders by wading chest high into the sea at Sandgate.

The south coast of England, having already been transformed into a giant army camp, now began to take on the appearance of a building site. Hundreds of navigators, or 'navvies' as they were more popularly known, were hired to dig the canal. This was hard work and it attracted hard men. The pay for a navigator was five shillings a week and, whilst the men spent their wages freely, to the delight of local traders, the attendant rise in crime and drunkenness was not so welcome. Nor perhaps were some of the social habits of the men, as depicted in a report in the Kentish Gazette of the 15th March 1805:

> Last week, the wife of one of the men employed in cutting the canal at Shorncliffe, was conducted by her husband to the market place, at Hythe, with a halter round her neck and tied to a post; from whence she was purchased for sixpence by a mulatto, the long drummer belonging to the band of the 4th regiment, lately at the barracks at that place-She was a young woman, apparently not more than 20 years of age, tall, and of a likely form and figure; her face, however, exhibited evident marks of incompatibility of temper; vulgarly, she had a pair of black eyes; notwithstanding this, the new partner led her away, with much apparent satisfaction from his bargain.

During the first few months of 1805, there were conflicting reports on the progress of the canal building. The Kentish Gazette on the 8th January 1805 was optimistic, describing the work being progressed *"With unexampled activity, at various places along the whole line…"*

In reality, a combination of inclement weather and organisational difficulties, especially with the civilian contractors, led to the work falling seriously behind schedule. In June, with work still proceeding at an unacceptable rate, Rennie was relieved of his duties and total responsibility for the project was passed back to Colonel Brown, with the work to be undertaken by a combination of troops and civilian contractors. The Royal Staff Corps, hitherto based in Chatham, was transferred to Hythe. These men were engineers and artificers and supervised the unskilled troops and labourers. By July Brown had nearly 1000 men working on the

canal, including two small militia regiments, the Cambridge and the Royal South Lincoln, which had been placed at his disposal. The troops were building the ramparts and turfing the banks, whilst the navvies continued to excavate the canal. To organise the movement of material and men along the canal and the military road, a detachment of men of the Royal Waggon Train was stationed at Hythe.

The Royal Waggon Train. The forerunner of today's Royal Logistics Corps, the RWT supplied the transport requirements during the construction of the canal.

The two projects sometimes came into conflict. With each of the Martello Towers requiring 500,000 bricks, the London brickfields soon found that they could not meet the demand. The abutments for the canal bridges were also intended to be made of bricks but, because there were none available, timber had to be used instead.

Unknown to the British, events were unfolding across the Channel; Napoleon was poised to strike. He had brought up his famed Imperial Guard and the cavalry. On the 20th July he issued the order for the invasion flotilla to be provisioned with all necessary artillery, powder and supplies, to enable it to sail at twenty-four hours notice. On the 3rd August he arrived in Boulogne to review the Army of England. In the belief that the West Indies strategy had rid him of the Royal Navy, the Emperor sent a despatch to Villeneuve on the 22nd August, commanding him to, *"Sail, do not lose a moment, and with my squadrons reunited enter the Channel. England is ours. We are ready and embarked. Appear for twenty-four hours, and all will be ended…"* To another of his admirals, Ganteaume, he commanded, *"Put to sea and sail here. We will avenge six centuries of insults and shame. Never have my soldiers on land and sea risked their lives for so great an object."* Napoleon's confidence is demonstrated by his invitation to the Vaudeville Theatre to move from Paris to Boulogne, ready to follow his triumphant soldiers into

The French flotilla at Boulogne. Ready to launch their invasion as soon as the Channel was clear of interference by the Royal Navy. The Kent coast, so near, yet so far.

London and to perform on the London stage.

Those few days during the summer of 1805 are probably as near to full scale invasion that the British Isles had been since 1066. Apart from Sir John Moore's men the English defences were woefully inadequate and, had the French arrived, they would have found, *"a shambles of partly built forts, barracks and Martello towers."*[4] But the French did not arrive. What Napoleon did not know was that Villeneuve, on his way back to France, had been mauled by the Royal Navy and, although he had escaped, the French admiral had sought the safe haven of Cadiz where he was trapped by the British fleet until, in October, he was driven out and to his doom at the Battle of Trafalgar.

By the time of the Duke of York's annual inspection of troops at Shorncliffe on 23rd August, there were rumours that Napoleon had given up his plans to invade and that the Army of England was preparing to leave Boulogne. Such rumours seem to have been well founded; during the last week of August, news reached Napoleon that his navy would not be coming, and he reluctantly gave orders for the Army of England to strike camp and march on Austria. The Emperor personally announced the decision to his men:

> BRAVE SOLDIERS OF THE BOULOGNE CAMP
> You are not going to England. The Emperor of Austria, bribed with English gold, has just declared war with France. Soldiers, new laurels await you beyond the Rhine; let us hasten to vanquish the enemies we have already conquered.

The news reached England after the capture of a French schooner on the 5th September. The following day the Hythe Gazette reported:

> All idea of invasion is now at an end. We learn that the camp at Boulogne has been broken up.

Invasion Medal. With the optimistic legend, Struck in London, Napoleon's dreams of marching through Kent to the capital were to remain unfulfilled.

England was safe and Napoleon's dreams of marching his victorious army through the streets of London dashed. The victory medal which had been recently struck in 1804, with the inscription: *Descente en Angleterre, frappe a Londres en 1804,* would never be pinned to a Frenchman's breast. The column that Napoleon's engineers had started to erect in 1804, just to the north of Boulogne, as a triumphal monument to the invasion army, was abandoned unfinished. It was completed only in 1840.

With the immediate threat of invasion over Sir John Moore hoped for a few days leave, but the Duke of York had other plans for him. The French having quit Boulogne, the Commander in

---

[4] As described by Sheila Sutcliffe in her book, *Martello Towers.*

Chief wanted to know the strength of the garrison remaining, and whether an invasion of France was viable. Moore's report advised caution and, when his views reached William Pitt, the Prime Minister agreed that invasion was out of the question. Despite this, the local press seem to have thought that some move on the French was afoot, reporting that,

> Major-General Moore's brigade at Shorncliffe, consisting
> of the First Battalions of the 43rd and 52nd (two, without
> exception, of the best disciplined battalions in the service),
> are under orders to embark, but wait their final orders till
> the arrival of Sir John who is at present in London.

Nelson's victory over the combined French and Spanish fleets at Trafalgar in October may have given the country cause for celebration, but the euphoria was all too short-lived. Early in 1806, the Emperor won the most outstanding battle of his career, at Austerlitz. Shortly after, on the 16th January, William Pitt died. It was said that the news of Austerlitz broke his spirit but, in truth, his health had been declining for some time and was not helped by his devotion to port, to which he was almost certainly addicted.

Sir John Moore was promoted to Lieutenant-General in October 1805 and, with the promotion, he bid farewell to Shorncliffe, moving on to duties in Sicily and Sweden. Late in 1808, Moore was placed in command of the twenty-five thousand strong British army sent to Portugal, and then into Spain to support Spanish resistance to the French army. With the arrival of French

The Retreat to Corunna, Spain. This 19th century picture shows General Moore leading his men on that terrible journey. In truth, Moore spent most of his time at the rear encouraging stragglers and organising the rearguard in fighting the French pursuit.

reinforcements, led by Napoleon himself, and the Spanish resistance having crumbled, General Moore had no option but to disengage and endeavour to save his army. He led his men on a merciless journey to Corunna, pursued all the way by the French. At Corunna, the British fleet arrived to take off the survivors, but not before a fierce battle that accounted for many British lives, including that of Sir John Moore himself.

In the immediate aftermath of Corunna, Sir John Moore was made the scapegoat of unfair and inaccurate political criticism. But enough people with influence, and knowledge of the true state of affairs in Spain, were prepared to speak out. In due course, Moore was given his rightful place as an honourable and heroic figure who, against the odds, had saved the majority of the British army from annihilation at the hands of a superior force. Perhaps the greatest testimonial to Moore was from Napoleon himself. The Emperor had entered Spain late in 1808 at the head of 300,000 of his best troops. His quarry was the small British army which he believed would retreat into Portugal, and from where he intended *"to hurl them into the sea"* and plant his French Eagles on the ramparts of Lisbon. But General Moore outflanked Napoleon and, despite being outnumbered by ten to one, he even threatened the French lines of communication, so that the Emperor himself had to retreat. Learning of the identity of his adversary, Napoleon wrote, *"Moore is the only General now worthy to contend with me. I shall now move against him in person."*

The legacy of Sir John Moore extended far beyond his gallantry at the battle of Corunna. As the Duke of Wellington himself acknowledged after Waterloo, the creation of the Light Infantry Brigade by Moore was perhaps the decisive factor in the defeat of Napoleon. In his History of the British Army, Fortescue wrote, *"No man, nor Cromwell, nor Marlborough nor Wellington has set so strong a mark for good upon the British Army as John Moore."* It was at Shorncliffe camp that this mark was first set.

One of the soldiers who served at Corunna, and who survived to tell the tale, was a humble private of the 1st Battalion of the elite 52nd Regiment. He was John Samuel Gough and, surviving the Peninsular Wars, he returned to his home and wife in Sandgate. Gough was born in 1777 at St Clements in London. After joining the army at the age of 22 he served first in the 27th Regiment of Foot, then the 40th before joining the 52nd at Shorncliffe. His son was John Bartholomew

The Gough's home. The two-roomed cottage in which the Goughs lived near to Sandgate Castle.

Gough, who, as a great Temperance speaker in America, became one of Sandgate's most famous sons.

The young Gough was sent to America at the age of 12 years with the promise of an apprenticeship. Although his parents were poor and they lived in a tiny two-roomed cottage in Sandgate, Gough later recalled his childhood enjoyment of the village fair on the green, next to the castle, with its merry-go-round and donkey races. The hopes of Gough's parents for his advancement in America did not materialise; the apprenticeship was not forthcoming and the boy became a poorly paid bookbinder. John's mother and sister joined him in America, but misfortune and tragedy struck when he lost his job and then his mother died. Unable to afford a decent burial, John became bitter and turned to drink. For thirteen years he lived a life of poverty and degradation caused by his alcohol abuse. Then, after hearing a temperance

John Samuel Gough. Proudly wearing his Military General Service Medal from the Napoleonic Wars.

speaker and signing the pledge, he gave up his habit and became a temperance orator himself. Gough travelled widely in America, giving an estimated 8,000 addresses and achieving worldwide fame, before his death in 1886. With fame came wealth, and Gough was able to buy a mansion house, Hillside, in Boylston, Massachusetts. He brought his father to America and was able to provide him with comfort in his declining years.

The old soldier had served the colours for 21 years before being wounded in the Peninsula Wars. He often talked of the famous battle of Corunna, where he witnessed Sir John Moore carried from the field fatally wounded, and then of the great General's burial on the night of the 16th January 1809, in a simple grave on the town's ramparts. Because the French forces were still nearby the General was buried in silence, wrapped only in his military cloak. In his autobiography, Gough described his father's sufferings during that awful retreat to Corunna, which were shared by many of his comrades,

J.S.Gough's MGS Medal. Gough's medal showing five clasps including that for Corunna.

I well remember my father saying to me, "John, you will never know what hunger is till you feel the two sides of your stomach grinding together." In that campaign, men mad with hunger fought like wolves over the half-decayed hoof of a bullock; and often when one of those poor animals, overcome with weakness and starvation, was staggering as if about to fall, the ready knife was applied to the throat, and the fainting soldiers, eagerly catching the blood in their hands, and hardly waiting for it to congeal, made it to take the place of food. In this retreat, the Fifty-second regiment became – to use the American expression – demoralized; and while they staggered on, my father threw himself out of the ranks, under the shadow of a large rock, to die; he could go no farther. Lying there, he took from his inner pocket a hymn-book (which I have today, with all the marks of its seventy years upon it), and began to read the hymn in which is the verse-

> When in the solemn hour of death
> I own Thy just decree,
> Be this the prayer of my last breath:
> O Lord, remember me.

He must die – it seemed inevitable – though far from home in a strange land. He was a Christian, and endeavoured to prepare himself for the change. Suddenly a large bird of prey, with a red neck growing out of a ruffle of feathers, came swooping along, almost brushing my

Sandgate High Street. Showing Gough's Soldiers Home on the left. The handsome clock can today be seen on the front of the Chichester Hall.

father's body with its wings; then circling up, he alighted on the point of the rock, and turned his blood-red eye on his intended victim.

As my father saw that horrible thing watching, and waiting to tear him in pieces even before life was extinct, it so filled him with horror and disgust that he cried, "I cannot endure this: it is too terrible. When I am unable to drive that fearful thing away, it will be tearing my flesh. I cannot endure it!" He rose to his feet and fell, then crawled and struggled away, till at length he crept into a poor hut, found safety, and soon after joined his regiment. Though he was very, very ill after that frightful episode, he recovered, and died in 1871, at the remarkable age of ninety-four years.

From this account of his father's labours, Gough's descriptive powers are evident, and it is little wonder that he succeeded as a public orator. During his life, John Bartholomew Gough returned to the place of his birth three times. His last

visit to Sandgate was in 1879, when he laid the corner stone to the J B Gough Soldiers Home, which also provided a temperance-inspired Coffee Tavern.

The Soldiers Home has long gone, although the building remains; now an antique shop it sits appropriately on the corner of Gough Road. As for Sir John Moore, today's visitor to Sandgate can see his memorial, unveiled by his great niece on the anniversary of his death in 1909. Its location, at the western end of Coastguard Cottages, is as near as possible to the house which Moore rented in Sandgate, on the site of which the cottages now stand. Less visible to the public is the statue and Memorial Library at Shorncliffe camp itself. Although the building is no longer used as a library, its unique stained glass windows remain as reminders of many of the outstanding army commanders and regiments of their day. Alongside a triple panel commemorating the 43rd, 52nd and 95th there are panels devoted to the 51st, the regiment which Moore joined

Sir John Moore Memorial, Sandgate. Unveiled in 1909, the memorial is a reminder of Moore's time at Shorncliffe, and his contribution to shaping of the modern British Army.

as a 16 year-old Ensign, and the 92nd, The Gordon Highlanders. As well as the window devoted to Sir John Moore, there are those remembering Kenneth MacKenzie, Lieutenant-Colonel Sydney Beckwith, Major-General Robert 'Black Bob' Crauford and Lieutenant-Colonel John Colborne. [5]The bronze statue of Moore stands high on a plinth, looking across the Sir John Moore Plain and beyond, over the Channel and to the coast of France, as if still alert for the first signs of invasion. Another permanent but, today, less well known tribute to Moore is the poem written by the Irish poet, Charles Wolfe. Published in 1820, and acclaimed by Byron as, *'The most perfect in the English language'*, the poem became a standard text for school children until the Great War produced its own collection of poetical works[6].

[5]A full description of the windows, together with photographs of them, can be found in 'A Short History of Shorncliffe Garrison' edited by Colin Caverhill (See Bibliography).

[6] The poem is reproduced in full in Appendix C.

Chapter 4

THE YEARS OF PEACE

After he quit the Camp of Boulogne, Napoleon continued to wage war across Europe for another ten years. Until his final defeat at Waterloo in 1815, Britain could not rest and the threat of renewed invasion attempts was ever present. Indeed, during 1811, the Emperor briefly flirted with the idea of restoring his invasion flotilla, which was still moored along the Picardy coast. Then, after his Grande Armee had perished on its withdrawal from Moscow in 1812, the idea was never spoken of again. The thousands of craft were left to rot and sink in the harbours and rivers of northern France.

The building of the Martello Towers and the Royal Military Canal continued well after the Army of England had left Boulogne, with the last of the south coast towers, of which there were 74, being completed in 1810. The Royal Military Canal was completed in 1809, although in the summer of 1806, by which time only six Martellos had been built, the Duke of York was able

Hythe and the Staff Barracks. In this fine 1820s engraving many features are shown. The barracks, the canal, the military road, the Royal Waggon Train quarters are all in the foreground. Twiss Fort, flanked by two Martello Towers, Sandgate Castle and two more towers are in the background.

to inspect a 19-mile stretch of the canal, from Hythe to Iden, from a small boat towed by relays of horses. The Royal Staff Corps, their work on the construction of the canal completed, remained in Hythe to operate and maintain the waterway. The barracks which they were allocated in Saltwood were not to their liking, so Colonel Brown set about finding a spot for permanent quarters. Land was purchased adjacent to the Military Road to the west of the town, on the landward side of the canal, and the Corps built their own set of barracks. Known simply as the Staff Barracks, the Corps took up residence in 1810. The two storey blocks were joined to the guardroom by arched walls and, to the rear and east, were single storey blocks. Additionally, a hospital was built, which had beds for forty patients, together with nurses' quarters and kitchens. In 1809, a house with a garden and a small field, just north of the new barracks, was purchased for the residence of the Commandant of the Corps; Colonel Brown moved into his quarters that June. The Royal Waggon Train, which had been brought in to transport the canal materials, by road and by barge, had also staked a claim and built their quarters on the opposite side of the canal to the Staff Barracks. The canal barges had to be drawn by horses, so the stabling, smithies and associated facilities had to be built. In the summer of 1812 there were 55 horses engaged in canal work, with 30 of them stabled in Hythe and the rest at Ham Street.

After the euphoria of victory at Waterloo in 1815 the country had to come to terms with peace for the first time in over twenty years. The prosperity and unity created by the effects of the war were soon revealed to be a thin veil, beneath which serious social problems lurked. Whilst the aristocracy continued to enjoy their prosperity, the rural and urban workers soon felt the effects of the change of times; clothing and arms for the army were no longer needed, and the thousands of soldiers who were discharged competed for the poorly paid work which, for many, did not generate even a subsistence wage. As the century progressed, these factors would lead to unrest, riots and, eventually, reform. The south coast of England between Brighton and Dover felt the immediate effects; the army barracks that had housed tens of thousands of militia and regular troops began to empty and the towns that had grown rich on supplying the needs of the soldiers had little to replace that trade. Little wonder that there was a resurgence in smuggling.

There is no doubt that the rise in popularity and prosperity of Sandgate, Folkestone and Hythe can be attributed to the wars with Napoleon, and that they also fell victim to the 'peace dividend'. In his *Rural Rides* in 1823, William Cobbett

Folkestone Seafront and Harbour. An 1830s engraving by E.W.Cooke. Although there is some minor development around St Eanswythe's Church, the town is still centred around the harbour. The picture suggests a time of smuggling and other dark deeds!

visited Folkestone and commented that it was then about a quarter of its size at the height of the Napoleonic wars. He also saw signs on the outskirts of the town of the post-war poverty with eighty-four men, women and children gleaning in a ten acre field, in other words scavenging for stalks of corn left after harvesting. By 1830 Folkestone was beginning to make attempts to attract civilian visitors. In his Watering Places of Great Britain, Hinton described the town,

> The bathing is good, the beach clean, and the machines very neat. Were some marine residences and lodging houses erected on the cliff, at the entrance from Sandgate, there is little doubt, but the number of bathing visitants would materially increase…There is a sad paucity of Marine Lodging-houses, for, with the exception of two or three in the Sandgate Road, and here and there one or two in the vicinity of the churchyard, there are scarcely any.

Apart from the lack of amenities there remained some serious drawbacks which Hinton had to acknowledge,

> The pier which forms a good promenade, is much frequented during the fine evenings; but some sad eyesores on the town side surround the harbour, comprising pig-styes, hovels and rookeries.

A decline in the number of troops at Shorncliffe and Hythe barracks was followed by a programme of disposal of surplus land and materials. As early as 1808 advertisements were appearing in the local press for the disposal of surplus land at the camp; initially 150 acres of training and exercise ground was let to local farmers for the grazing and feeding of cattle. The Kentish Gazette gave notice of an auction sale to be held on the 28th October 1816, consisting of part of the barracks including *"one range of officers houses and three ditto of soldiers barracks with cleaning sheds and other outbuildings."* On the other hand, the army clearly intended to remain at Shorncliffe, as seen from a notice in the local newspaper on the 18th August 1818, *"The barracks at Shorncliffe, hitherto temporary, are now rendered permanent, brick being substituted for weather-boarding on the exterior and the whole are undergoing a thorough repair."*

But even during this period of contraction in the size and importance of Shorncliffe there continued to be occasional field days that provided a welcome and grand spectacle for the local population. As well as military drills, there were entertainments from the regimental bands, both on and off camp. The Kentish Gazette of 1814 reported in glowing terms of a fete champetre held at the Cherry Garden in Folkestone on the 18th July of that year, at which the music was provided by the band of the 95th Rifles.

> The tables, ornamented in the most rural manner, were placed under the shade of the trees, whose thick foliage prevented the too ardent rays of the sun from penetrating.

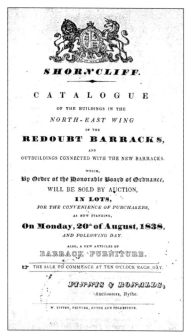

SHORNCLIFF.

C A T A L O G U E

OF THE BUILDINGS IN THE

N O R T H - E A S T W I N G

OF THE

REDOUBT BARRACKS,

AND

OUTBUILDINGS CONNECTED WITH THE NEW BARRACKS.

WHICH,

By Order of the Honorable Board of Ordnance,

WILL BE SOLD BY AUCTION,

IN LOTS,

FOR THE CONVENIENCE OF PURCHASERS,

AS NOW STANDING,

On Monday, 20ᵗʰ of August, 1838,

AND FOLLOWING DAY.

ALSO, A FEW ARTICLES OF

BARRACK FURNITURE.

☞ THE SALE TO COMMENCE AT TEN O'CLOCK EACH DAY.

TIPPIN & RONALDS,

Auctioneers, Hythe.

W. TIPPEN, PRINTER, HYTHE AND FOLKESTONE.

Auction of Redoubt Barracks. August 1838. With the country at peace, the Board of Ordnance was selling off the nort-east wing of the barracks, together with its furniture.

The mild southern breeze gently fanned the leaves, and produced a sensation of the most agreeable freshness. The view of the Roman works on the surrounding hills, the woods, the sea, with the distant view of the coast of France, all combined to render this one of the most desirable spots for such an occasion. About four o'clock, upwards of forty ladies and gentlemen sat down to an elegant dinner consisting of every delicacy which the season could afford. The band of the Corps attended, and played many select airs.

In his survey of Cheriton in 1828, John Adams noted that there were 3 sets of barracks at Shorncliffe; Cavalry, Infantry and Redoubt Barracks, the last overlooking Hospital Hill, where there was a small hospital. But the decline continued and, in 1838, the buildings and furniture at Redoubt Barracks were put up for auction followed, the next year, by materials, surplus barrack furniture and utensils of the Infantry Barracks. A sudden increase in the population at Shorncliffe camp in July 1849 proved very unpopular locally, as described in the Maidstone and South Eastern Gazette,

> Much anxiety has been felt during the past week by the inhabitants of Folkestone and Sandgate, at the report that 500 convicts from Millbank Penitentiary were to be located at Shorncliff barracks on account of the increase in cholera at that prison. Upon enquiry, we find that there are no grounds whatsoever for alarm, as only the most healthy of the convicts will be brought here. About 100 arrived by special train on Saturday morning last at Coolinge Bridge near Folkestone, and were marched off to the barracks which had been prepared for their reception…The barracks are on an eminence, and entirely isolated. A more healthy spot could not be selected.

Whether the residents of Folkestone and Sandgate were reassured by this report is another matter.

Along the coast at Hythe there was a similar picture. The bustle that the presence of the military brought to the town began to fade as the Napoleonic wars came to an end. At one time there was even a horse-racing track at Hythe. In June 1813 the garrison races boasted five events each run between two horses with a prize of fifty guineas. The Royal Staff Corps had built its own set of barracks in 1810; known simply as the 'Staff Barracks', they were described by W. H. Ireland in 1829 as a handsome range of buildings. Brought to Hythe to supervise the construction and then the maintenance of the Royal Military Canal, the cost of retaining the Corps in peacetime could not be justified and, in 1838, they were disbanded. After their departure, Hythe Barracks continued to be used, but on a much more irregular basis. In 1842 a detachment of the 29th Regiment were given a temporary home there after their transport ship was wrecked on the Dymchurch Wall. Several other regiments were stationed there including, during the early 1850s, troops sent daily to Shorncliffe camp as sentries when, as an annexe to Fort Pitt in Chatham, it was used to confine lunatics.

Although never called upon to impede Napoleon's invading army, the Royal Military Canal had proved useful during the Napoleonic Wars for transporting troops; in 1809 troops returning from Spain, who would have previously faced a two-day march back to Kent, were towed along the canal from the River Rother to Hythe in just four hours. In 1810, with the prospect of invasion

Royal Military Canal c 1830. Scanlon's Bridge crosses the canal with St Leonard's Church in the background. After the end of the Napoleonic Wars, the canal was also used for commercial traffic. The artist for this scene was standing at Gallows Corner.

having receded, the canal was opened to the public with a regular barge service plying between Hythe and Rye. A passenger service was operated between the Swan in Hythe and Appledore; the outward journey leaving at 10.30 am and returning at 5.00 pm each day. In the same year, Ladies' Walk was laid out to commemorate the jubilee of George III. Running from the canal to the shore this footpath was joined by Ladies' Bridge in 1813, thus providing direct access from the town to the seafront. Despite these efforts to encourage use of the canal the tolls recovered simply did not begin to cover the costs of maintenance and, in 1838, the Royal Staff Corps was replaced by a detachment of two sergeants and forty men of the Royal Sappers and Miners. Even this much reduced military involvement was further reduced so that, by 1841, there was none at all. The Royal Waggon Train had also quit its quarters on the opposite bank of the canal and, in February 1841, there was an auction sale of its residue of building materials and 'unserviceable stores', including elm trees. Elms

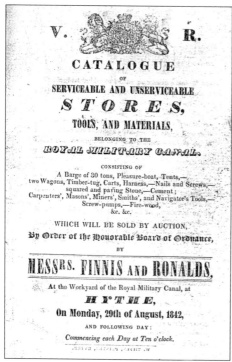

V.   **R.**

CATALOGUE

OF

SERVICEABLE AND UNSERVICEABLE

STORES,

TOOLS, AND MATERIALS,

BELONGING TO THE

ROYAL MILITARY CANAL.

CONSISTING OF

A Barge of 30 tons, Pleasure-boat, Tents,—
two Wagons, Timber-tug, Carts, Harness,—Nails and Screws,—
squared and paving Stone,—Cement ;
Carpenters', Masons', Miners', Smiths', and Navigator's Tools,—
Screw-pumps,—Fire-wood,
&c. &c.

WHICH WILL BE SOLD BY AUCTION,

By Order of the Honourable Board of Ordnance,

BY

MESSRS. FINNIS AND RONALDS,

At the Workyard of the Royal Military Canal, at

HYTHE,

On Monday, 29th of August, 1842,

AND FOLLOWING DAY :

Commencing each Day at Ten o'clock.

Auction of Canal Stores. August 1842. A miscellany of items to be sold. The auctioneers were again Finnis & Ronalds.

had been planted along the banks of the canal to provide stability and these were, presumably, surplus to requirements. To complete this rash of auction sales of military miscellanea, a two-day sale took place at the Workyard of the Royal Military Canal in August 1842. Amongst the items on sale were a 30-ton barge and a pleasure boat.

The decline in the canal's fortunes was compounded by the opening of the railway line between Ashford and Hastings in 1851, providing connections at Appledore and Rye. Although ownership of the canal remained with the Crown, it ceased to have any military value and, apart from modest income derived from the renting of land to farmers for grazing their sheep, it had no real economic value either. With an average annual tonnage of 13,000 between the years 1841-1850, barge traffic was earning only £300 per year.

Other than a brief period of military duty during the Crimean War, when the War Department took it over, the canal had become a liability and, in 1868, the government decided to sell the canal and the military road to a commercial concern. On hearing of this, the Lords and Bailiff of Romney Marsh stepped in with a bid and managed to secure agreement for a 999-year lease of the canal between Iden and Shorncliffe. The Corporation of Hythe were not happy with this arrangement, and petitioned for a Bill to give it control of that part of the Canal which passed through the borough. After some heated debate, the Bill was passed, and Hythe took control of the Canal between West Hythe and Shorncliffe. Interestingly, the War Department retained rights, which it still enjoys, for, *"Pontooning and for all other military exercises and evolutions together with the right to place military stores and tents thereon."*

As with the Royal Military Canal, the Martello

Martello Tower, Folkestone. A pen and ink sketch by Henry Moses, probably showing tower number 3. One of a series drawn during the 1840s. (WD)

Towers were never called upon to prove themselves against Napoleon. So what became of them? For the most part no immediate use could be found and many were abandoned by the military, slipping gently into neglect and decay. Writing from the safety of ten years after Napoleon had been routed, William Cobbett came across the towers on his Rural Rides:

> I had baited my horse at New Romney, and was coming jogging along very soberly, now looking at the sea, then looking at the cattle, then the corn, when, my eye, in swinging round, lighted upon a great round building, standing upon the beach. I had scarcely had time to think about what it could be, when twenty or thirty others, standing along the coast, caught my eye; and, if any one had been behind me, he might have heard me exclaim, in a voice that made my horse bound, "The Martello Towers by...!" Oh, Lord! To think that I should be destined to behold these monuments to the wisdom of Pitt and Dundas and Percival! Good God! Here they are, piles of bricks in a circular form, about three hundred feet (guess) circumference at the base, about forty feet high and about one hundred and fifty feet circumference at the top. There is a door-way, about midway up, in each, and each has two windows. Cannons were to be fired from the top of these things, in order to defend the country against the Jacobins!
>
> I think I have counted upwards of thirty of these ridiculous things, which, I dare say, cost five, perhaps ten, thousand pounds each; and one of which was, I am told, sold on the coast of Sussex, the other day for Two Hundred Pounds!

It is true that, at the time Cobbett was writing, the country was still suffering the economic consequences of years of war. The Martello Towers and Royal Military Canal were easily identified as white elephants and became the target of much criticism. Bearing in mind that Cobbett, the ex sergeant-major, had become a Radical he may, nevertheless, have spoken for many when describing the towers and canal as *"pauper-making work...some of the causes that are now sending some farmers to the workhouse and driving others to flee the country or to cut their throats!"* He noted with disapproval that, *"These very towers are now used to keep these loyal Cinque Ports themselves in order! These towers are now used to lodge men, whose business it is to sally forth, not upon the Jacobins, but upon smugglers!"*

Cobbett's apparent sympathy for the smugglers was by no means unique. Even during the wars with France, this clandestine trade had continued but there is no

Sandgate c 1850. An engraving by George Cruikshank. The structure to the left of the picture is Martello Tower number 4. Others can be seen on the hills and along the shoreline in the distance.

doubt that, with the hardship of the post-war years, more people were tempted to fall in with the smugglers. This included a number of former soldiers who had been discharged at the end of the conflict and who had little prospect of finding work. One of the area's most notorious smuggling enterprises, the Aldington Gang, was said to have recruited a number of such men. John Gough's father resisted any temptation to join the gang; he knew that, at the very least, his small army pension would be liable to be forfeit if he did. It must have been difficult for Gough senior to stay aloof when all around seemed to be taking their share of this profitable trade. The younger Gough, who was born in Sandgate the year after Waterloo, has left us with a detailed account of these times:

> There was a regularly organised gang of [smugglers] in the village; and I must confess that the sympathies of nearly the whole community were generally with them, though their influence was fearfully demoralizing. Lying close to the sea – only twenty-two miles from the French coast with high hills surrounding the village on every side but one that towards Hythe – it was a spot peculiarly fitted for their successful exploits against the Revenue. They were a bold, hardy set of men. A public house, called the Fleur-de-Lis, was their favourite haunt. Their boats, painted white, lay along the beach. Every one knew they were smugglers – even the men-of-war's men knew them – but the difficulty was to catch them. Every man in the village

Smugglers caught in the act. Based on a painting by J.W.M.Turner, this 1826 engraving finds smugglers off Folkestone's beach having to hand their contraband over to the Revenue men.

who was engaged in defrauding the Revenue, had a nickname...Some of these nicknames in Sandgate were Bonum, Crappie, Horny, Boxer and Stickeroff. The name decscended from father to son.

The Martello Towers were used at this time for the accommodation of the men-of-war's men, with their officers, whose duty it was to pace the beach, day and night , armed with cutlass and pistols...

The most perilous part of the smuggler's work is to land the goods; and it is surprising how successful they were – so many were helping them on the shore. Horses were waiting to carry their goods up the country, and a gang of men ready to wade into the water, and sling a couple of ankers, or cases on their shoulders and run up the beach...Occasionally they had trouble, and father would say, when we have heard firing, and sometimes the rushing of feet past our door, - *"Ah! The smugglers are at it again."*

One circumstance I well remember. A young man had bought a couple of pounds of tea for his mother, and had put it into his long fishing boots; on landing, the preventive officer insisted on searching him personally, for, he said, *"I smell tea."* He was resisted, and the quarrel

Martello Tower number 3. Another Moses sketch dated August 10th 1844. Could that be Mrs Sweetman's washing hanging out to dry? (WD)

grew into such a height, that the officer drew his pistol and shot the young man dead. In one minute the unfortunate officer was cut to pieces; a dozen knives were used upon him; and, I believe, not one of the men was punished, though the deed was done in broad daylight. The men engaged in the affray were not seen for some time after in the village, and woe be to anyone who would

Martello Towers at West Hythe. This picture dates from late 19th Century. The two foremost towers can still be seen. Most of the others have been destroyed by either the sea or the military.

have betrayed them; his life would not have been worth a button.

In 1830, four years after Cobbett had written them off, the Martello Towers were rearmed with thirty-two pounders in the face of a renewed threat from France. In 1845, as revolution again descended upon France with the toppling of Louis XVIII, invasion was again threatened and the Prime Minister, the Duke of Wellington, considered the towers to have a useful role as *'excellent defensive guard house(s).'* Again, in 1859, the towers were brought back into service when Emperor Napoleon III was fomenting trouble in Europe[7].

Between their periods of duty in defending the country from possible invasion many other uses have been found for the towers. As we have seen they were used by the Revenue during the early 19th century in their fight against the traditional south coast occupation of smuggling, then as signalling stations for passing naval and military messages using semaphore devices erected on the tops of the towers. Some became retirement homes for old soldiers who, in return, kept the towers ventilated in an attempt to deter the onset of dry rot in the oak floors. Census records reveal a succession of occupants of Martello Tower number 3 on Folkestone's East Cliff. George Sweetman, a Coastguard, lived there with his wife in 1851, and they were still there in 1861. In 1871 it was Arthur Porter, a Royal Artillery Gunner, with his wife and two daughters. By 1881 it was the Coastguard again in occupation, with Henry Mather, his wife and their baby son. During the 1890s the Finn family moved in and they caused something of a stir in 1898 during their daughter's wedding. After the service at the Parish Church the families returned to the Tower for the reception and marked the happy event by discharging the rooftop cannon. The people of Folkestone rushed out of their homes, believing this to be a signal that the French were about to attack!

Gradually, however, the military uses became fewer and the towers were allowed to slip into disuse and decay. Those within the Hythe Ranges were used for range finding and target practice and even for testing explosives. Some were sold and have become homes, cafes, museums and scout headquarters. At times of war, many have been drafted back into martial use; during the Second World War they became part of the scheme of coastal defence, which was particularly fitting as Hitler's invasion plans bore a marked similarity to those of Napoleon. Today, a number of surviving towers can still be seen along the south coast. The only one that remains in its original Napoleonic condition is Number 24 at Dymchurch and which, during summer weekends, is open to the public. After two hundred years, the Martello Towers remain as resolute as ever and provide a stark reminder of just how close the British Isles came to invasion by Napoleon's Army of England.

After the years of relative decline at Shorncliffe camp and Hythe barracks, the 1850s saw the dawn of a new era. Since the end of the Napoleonic Wars the size of Britain's standing army had been reduced and barrack accommodation had fallen

---

[7] See chapter 7 for further details of the events of 1859.

from 95,000 beds at the turn of the 19th century to just 21,000 in 1854. This state of affairs was reflected locally and, apart from the brick-built Staff Barracks at Hythe and some permanent structures at Shorncliffe, the timber buildings had become dilapidated through lack of use and poor maintenance. The events that reversed this decline were the outbreak of the Crimean War in March 1854, and the arrival of the School of Musketry at Hythe in 1853.

Chapter 5

THE CRIMEAN WAR AND THE MERCENARIES

In 1853 the Crimean Peninsula, situated in the Black Sea, was the scene of ambitions by the Russian Empire over territory belonging to the Ottoman Empire (now Turkey). Great Britain and France joined forces with Sardinia and the Ottomans to resist this unacceptable shift in the European balance of power and war was declared on Russia on the 28th March 1854. Two months later, Lord Raglan set sail for the Crimea with 30,000 troops, eventually arriving there in September. Over the course of the next two months, the British army suffered heavy losses in three infamous battles; River Alma, Balaklava (the scene of the Charge of the Light Brigade) and Inkerman. The British had entered the war some 40,000 men under strength and the losses during that first winter, due more to the appalling conditions suffered by the men than to battle, were catastrophic. With the siege of Sebastapol underway, to remain an effective fighting force in the

The Crimean War. A soldier of the Rifle Brigade preparing for sentry duty. The troops were ill-equipped for the harsh winter conditions. This man had to take the boots of the sentry he was relieving. The army urgently needed men to replace those lost through battle or illness.

peninsular and to fulfil its obligations to her allies, the country desperately needed to recruit more men.

Since the enlightened days of Sir John Moore, the ethos in the army had returned to the inhumane regime of the 18th century. Even the great Duke of Wellington had said of his men, *"They are nothing but scum",* and little had changed in the years since Waterloo. Pay was still poor and the lash continued to be applied as liberally as it had in the days of Rifleman Harris. Consequently, a life serving the colours was not an attractive proposition. In any event it was established military thinking that it took two years to train a soldier for battle, and the government did not have two years to spare.

Faced with the same crisis as 50 years earlier, and in a curious replay of history, the government first sought to entice men from the county militias into the regular army. The militia troops had only signed up to fight on British soil and showed no great interest in going off to the Crimea. The solution was to recruit soldiers from abroad. During the Napoleonic wars the British had recruited foreign troops; most notable was the King's German Legion. They were Hanoverian soldiers who, after their country's conquest by Napoleon, came to England to reform and return to the European mainland as an effective fighting force. This they did with great distinction.

Despite initial political and public resistance to the idea of foreign recruiting for the Crimean campaign, necessity won the day. Initial attempts were made to attract recruits in America but these were disappointing, but more success was had on mainland Europe. A total of nine thousand men were enlisted with the offer of a bounty and employment for the duration of the war. Unlike the soldiers of the King's German Legion, these men did not join up through patriotic fervour; they were mercenaries.

Mercenaries at Shorncliffe. To house the foreign troops wooden huts were erected at Shorncliffe camp.

Initially, they were all known as the Foreign Legion but, at Queen Victoria's insistence, they were renamed to show their membership of the British Army, and with due regard to their main country of origin. The British German Legion (the BGL) was to be garrisoned and trained at Shorncliffe, the British Swiss Legion was based at Dover, and the British Italian Legion was stationed at Aldershot. To house the BGL rows of wooden barracks had to be hastily erected and these were finished just before a Royal inspection in August 1855. In addition to the barracks, also built were a church, a house for the commandant, three schools and houses for their masters and five canteens, erected by the Hythe brewery firm of Mackesons.

The BGL was organised into the cavalry of the 1st and 2nd Light Dragoons, three Rifle (or Jager) Battalions and five Light Infantry Battalions. Most of the officers and men were Prussian, but many other nationalities were represented, including some British. The uniforms and equipment of the Legionnaires were similar to British Army issue of the time; light infantry wore red frock tunics and grey trousers with a white belt and a heavy fur cap. Riflemen carried a continental style knapsack with the flap folded over the greatcoat. Writing to his home in Prussia, Rifleman Gustav Steinbart described his uniform as *"...black from head to toe...with two small rows of black horn buttons on the black tunic."* Generally regarded as 'crack' troops, the Legion riflemen were armed with the Minie rifle. Bandsmen of all foot regiments wore white tunics with red plumes in their shakos. No doubt, to keep a tight control on the purse strings, it was invariably the case that the battalion paymasters were British officers. Many of the men had military training and experience of warfare and soon the sound of mock battles once again echoed throughout the countryside around Shorncliffe camp. At the end of the day's training the troops would march back to camp singing their national songs.

The presence of the BGL was initially welcomed by the local communities, bringing trade and a degree of elegance and mystery to the area. Marianne Merriton was one young woman seduced by the romantic lure of an attachment to a Legionnaire, and it landed her in court. She had become infatuated with Lieutenant Augustus Lewis of the 1st Jager corps of the German Legion. She left her parent's home to live with

Singing Legionnaires. A contemporary newspaper sketch showing Legionnaires relaxing after a day's training.

Lewis and, when he left for the Crimea, she followed him there. Before returning to England they were married in a Lutheran ceremony which, unknown to Marianne, was not recognised by the English Church. Back in England, he put her in lodgings in Sandgate under the name of Mrs. Lewis. When Lewis was transferred to Colchester, he broke off the relationship with Marianne, leaving her penniless and homeless. One evening in August 1856, having followed him to Colchester, Marianne saw Lewis walking with *'a girl of loose character'* and she scratched the officer's face during an altercation. She appeared in court charged with the assault. The News of the World reported that, after hearing the whole sorry tale from the poor woman's lawyer, *"Taking into account all the circumstances and the provocation and unkindness the young woman had experienced at the hands of Lewis, they could not do otherwise than dismiss the complaint, which they did with the most perfect disgust."* The verdict was received by those in the public gallery with a burst of applause.

The BGL regiments had their own bands, and concerts were held in Folkestone and Hythe for the enjoyment of the local populace. At a concert in October 1855 at Hythe Town Hall the audience was delighted that the evening's

Concert Poster. Advertising a concert at Hythe Town Hall on the 10th October 1855. The last item on the programme is a polka dedicated to the ladies of the town.

entertainment closed with a polka dedicated to the ladies of the town.

To add to the popularity of the Legion, their presence attracted a Royal visit in the summer of 1855. At lunchtime on the 9th August, Queen Victoria and Prince Albert arrived at Folkestone Harbour railway station. A short carriage ride brought the Royal party to the Pavilion Hotel, which had been festooned with flags, and, after taking refreshment there, the journey resumed[8]. After turning into Undercliff where a triumphal arch had been erected and covered with evergreens, the procession continued along the Lower Sandgate Road, into Sandgate where, according to The Illustrated London News,

> The quiet little village, which has lately roused into the most unusual action by the Camp in its vicinity, was not behindhand in offering a welcome to the Sovereign. Triumphal arches spanned its only street and every house displayed the loyalty of its owner by exhibiting flags or evergreens.

Queen Victoria at Shorncliffe. 9th August, 1855. The royal couple reviewing the BGL at Folkestone. From The Illustrated London News.

The royal party turned into Military Road and the climb to Shorncliffe camp where they were to review the five thousand troops of the British German Legion, and those of the British Swiss Legion who had travelled from Dover for the occasion. The Queen was wearing a dress of blue and white, with a white bonnet and, as the royal party entered the camp, three bands all began to play the National Anthem, each in a different key! After the review, during which the Queen and Prince Albert spoke to many of the troops in their native German, the visitors inspected the huts, which had been decorated with bunting for the occasion. The day was rounded off with dinner in the mess of the 1st Infantry Regiment, paid for by the officers. To celebrate the event one Sandgate bard penned the following verses, which were to be sung to the tune of 'God Save the Queen'.

> "Brightly the sun looks down
> On our delighted town,
> All hearts beat high
> Terrace and tower are gay,
> And Shorncliff's heights display

[8] Thereafter the hotel became the Royal Pavilion Hotel.

Unwonted scenes today-
Our Queen comes nigh.

"With swelling hearts elate
The foreign troops await
Thy visit here.
Thy presence will inspire
Their breasts with fresh desire,
And fan the martial fire
Enkindled there.

"Victoria's smile shall cheer,
Her gentle word endear
Her memory.
And should they leave this shore
To visit us no more,
Amid the cannon's roar
They'll think of thee.

"Honoured by Royalty,
Raised from obscurity,
Sandgate is seen.
We now our voices raise,
Each heart its homage pays,
While each devoutly prays
'God save the Queen.' "

Whilst the Queen and Prince Albert were able to speak to the Legionnaires in German, not everyone had that advantage. When one German soldier went into a shop in Hythe (BGL troops were also encamped just to the west of Hythe) and asked for *"something for a soup"*, the shopkeeper helpfully displayed a large selection of ingredients. With each item came the

The British German Legion in Hythe. The Legion had a camp at the Roughs in Hythe as well as at Shorncliffe. This contemporary picture from The Illustrated London News tends to exaggerate the grandeur of the cliffs.

response, *"Nicht for ze soup."* The soldier then hit on the idea of drawing a sketch and down into the cellar went the shopkeeper emerging with a fistful of birch brooms. Crestfallen, the soldier realised that he was not going to be understood, and he left the shop empty-handed. The sequel to the tale was that, some twenty years later, a Mr Delhaye, a wholesale confectioner from Dover, visited the same shop with the same shopkeeper. His brother, it transpired, had been the disappointed customer. What he had intended his diagram to convey was that, for his soup, he had wanted *a head of celery!*

It may have been language difficulties that led to an unfortunate incident early in 1856. Following an accident a bottle of aconite had been damaged and an orderly at Shorncliffe was taking it to be used as lamp fuel. Legionnaire Ferdinand Schutze saw the orderly carrying the crimson liquid and, thinking it was rum, asked for a drink. He was told not to touch it as it was a poison but, heedless of the advice, he drank it as did another soldier. Despite medical attention, Schutze died and his comrade was not expected to survive. An inquest returned a verdict of accidental death. The same coroner's inquest, held in the mess room at Shorncliffe, had to investigate the death of another Legionnaire. After the sound of a gunshot in the barrack room, Private Ferdinand Albauns of the 2nd Jager Regiment was found with his head partly blown away and he died within 15 minutes. Albauns had been reduced from sergeant to private and this had played on his mind to such an extent that he confided in one witness that, *"He would destroy himself, as he considered honour before everything."* The coroner's verdict was that *"the deceased had destroyed himself, being then in a state of temporary insanity."*

The Legionnaires were not well fed and a number of unscrupulous local tradesmen took full advantage by overcharging troops looking to supplement their diets. Two soldiers, however, decided to help themselves by using their bayonets to steal loaves from a Sandgate baker's window. On parade the following morning, not a single soldier was missing his bayonet, despite those being used for liberating the bread being left in the shop. Cases were reported of sheep being stolen from local farms, then being killed and roasted in secrecy. This caused such anxiety in the area that it was suggested that a body of London policeman should be called in. But when the men did try to become self-sufficient, local interests intervened; a private beershop was opened by the camp surgeon, Dr. Hartmann, but it was quickly closed after complaints about the competition from local innkeepers.

During 1856 the Legionnaires became increasingly discontented and they began deserting by the score. The constabulary of

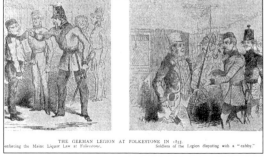

THE GERMAN LEGION AT FOLKESTONE IN 1855.
enforcing the Maine Liquor Law at Folkestone.   Soldiers of the Legion disputing with a "cabby."

Trouble in Folkestone. These newspaper cartoons show that, sometimes, the Legionnaires received bad press.

Folkestone, consisting of five constables and an inspector, were hard pressed to deal with the rising number of cases of drunkenness and disorder. A minor riot occurred in February 1856, when two Legionnaires had been arrested for stealing and placed in Folkestone gaol. Their crime was having sold ill-fitting army boots, a practice generally adopted and considered as a perk. The authorities thought otherwise and decided to make an example of the two men. Fifty of their comrades descended on the town and tried to storm the gaol, and only with difficulty did the small military picket stationed in the Town Hall manage to disperse them. Shortly afterwards, their ranks swelled by more Legionnaires, the rescuers returned and order was only restored with the arrival of a cavalry detachment. Other symptoms of the men's disaffection were a steady rise in the incidence of illness and even suicide. The camp hospital was kept busy with a range of conditions but, during the summer of 1855, an outbreak of cholera put the medical facilities under considerable strain. Only the previous year Sandgate had been hit by the disease leading to the deaths of 48 people. Although the new outbreak at the camp was contained, this was not before 13 soldiers had lost their lives. The incident was investigated and found to have been due to the questionable practice of the men throwing their filth down the wells from which they drew their drinking water.

Although there was a steady and increasing incidence of anti-social behaviour from some of the Legionnaires, an event in 1856 was altogether in a different league. Private Dedea Redanies was attached to the British Swiss Legion when he met eighteen year-old Caroline Back, whose mother took in the laundry for the men of the Legion. One evening in May, Redanies visited Caroline and invited her to Shorncliffe camp, ostensibly to meet his brother. Mrs Back was hesitant, but gave her permission provided Caroline's sixteen year old sister, Maria, accompanied them. Thus, the trio set out on foot early on the Sunday morning for the 10 mile walk to Folkestone. Eventually they came to the outskirts of Folkestone, approaching the Valliant Sailor inn, to a secluded spot known locally as Steddy Hole, and it was here that Redanies suggested they should rest for a while. The Legionnaire then produced a dagger and stabbed Maria several times in the chest before turning his attention to Caroline and plunged the blade into her. Taking their shawls, he left the bodies in the grass verge where a passing carpenter, Thomas Girling, discovered them. Dr William Bateman was called to the scene where he examined the bodies and found that Maria, who still wore her gloves and bonnet, had four stab wounds to her chest and that her dress was soaked in blood. Caroline had been stabbed three times but it was also clear that she had put up a fight as her hands were badly lacerated.

After the wretched deed, Redanies set off on foot for Canterbury, pausing long enough at Lower Hardres to compose and send a letter of confession to the girls' mother and another to his commanding officer. The following day he was seen by George Fryer, 'constable and labourer', in the village of Chartham and, as the policeman approached him, Redanies again brought out his knife. But, instead of

Sentence of Death. The court extract of the trial of Dedea Redanies. It records that, having confessed to the murders, he is to be "Hanged by the neck until he be dead" and his body then to be buried within the precincts of Maidstone Gaol.

using it against the officer, he turned it upon himself. Redanies managed to stab himself three times before he was disarmed and, taken to the Kent and Canterbury hospital, his life hung in the balance for several days. After his recovery, Redanies was kept locked up in Folkestone gaol until his case was heard at Maidstone Assizes later in the year. His letter to Mrs. Back, which had been recovered from the post office, was read out to the court. It seems that he suspected that Caroline's affections for him were waning, and as he then recorded, *"...the unhappy thought came into my head that Caroline rather may die from my hands than to allow [her] love to be bestowed upon others."*[9] The British public were enthralled by details of Redanies' terrible crime with its undertones of unrequited love, and the national newspapers gave regular updates on the Legionnaire's recovery from his self-inflicted wounds and his subsequent trial. The sad tale culminated in the soldier's conviction for double murder and Dedea Redanies was hanged on New Year's Day 1857 from the scaffold on top of the porter's lodge at Maidstone Prison in front of a crowd of five thousand. The Redanies' incident was immortalised in a ballad, variously entitled, 'The Folkestone Murder' or 'Maria and Sweet Caroline' and was often heard sung at pubs and Gypsy gatherings during the early twentieth century[10].

It is impossible to know how the inhabitants of Folkestone, Sandgate and Hythe felt about the Legionnaires. Certainly their money was welcome, but the incidents of lawlessness would have caused consternation. Writing in the 1930s Charles Igglesden, in his 'Saunters Through Kent', paused at Sandgate and described one incident involving Legionnaires in the following uncompromising terms:

> The Foreign Legion stationed at Shorncliffe Camp, consisted of the scallywags of the Continent, mainly Germans, and intense hatred existed between them and the peace-loving people of Sandgate. The feud sometimes resulted in street fighting of the old-fashioned sort, and the Legionnaires usually came off second when they reeled about the streets in small batches. One Saturday night, however, a pitched battle took place, all the young bloods of Sandgate, aided by a few bearded veterans, lying in wait for the enemy. But, as in warfare, their strategy was frustrated by the action of a spy, and down came the furious Legionnaires in great numbers. The fight in the

[9] See Appendix D for the full text of Redanies' letter to Mrs Back. [10] See Appendix E for the lyrics of the ballad.

open was short and sharp; the civilians were driven into the side streets, and many a skull was cracked, many a nose made to bleed, and teeth were knocked out before the foreigners started to return in triumph to the camp. But the lights in the bar of the Military Inn attracted them; they had already smelt blood and those bottles on the shelf were at their mercy. Into the bar they rushed, leapt the counter, and in a few minutes not a bottle of liquor was left. Up the hill they staggered, draining bottles as they went. No one exactly knew the sequel, but the Foreign Legion found Sandgate out of bounds for a month, and the tradesmen had the worst of the duel, for whilst they were nursing bruised bodies and healing wounds they suffered the loss of the Legionary trade during those four weeks.

Whilst the incident described by Igglesden may well have occurred, his interpretation of it, and of the general feelings of the folk of Sandgate towards the Legionnaires, may have been coloured by the fact that he was writing soon after the Great War, at a time when anti-German feeling was still high. Difficult as it is to glean the true feelings of the local population some 150 years later, if contemporary newspaper reports are a reflection of that feeling, then the general attitude would seem to have been a positive one. The Legion was always ready to turn out at times of trouble; when a fire broke out at a farm in Cheriton in March 1856 the Folkestone Chronicle reported,

Legionnaire and his wife. There are very few photographs of the Legionnaires. This shows an officer with the rank of Captain.

Too much praise cannot be given to the soldiers of the Cavalry, the 2nd regiment of Rifles and the 4th regiment of Infantry of the British German Legion who…were early at the scene of the destruction and exerted themselves strenuously in working the engines from the camp.

There can be no doubt that the presence of the BGL added colour to local life, but these foreign soldiers had been recruited to fight for the British and her allies in the Crimea. In October 1855 the first contingent of nine hundred men of the BGL destined for the Crimea was marched to Folkestone Junction Station. Large crowds turned out to see them leave, amongst them was a servant girl, perhaps waving farewell to her sweetheart, who stumbled over the cliff edge on the Leas and fell to her death. By the time the Legions arrived in the Crimea the fighting was all but over; the Treaty of Paris had been signed and an armistice was declared in March 1856, and the Legionnaires now had to return to England without having fired a shot. However, a number of the men who had arrived at Scutari (where Florence Nightingale acquired her fame) contracted cholera and died before they could be brought back to England.

With the end of the Crimean war, Shorncliffe camp was needed for the returning British soldiers, and there arose the thorny question of what to do with the Legionnaires. The majority of the men could not return to their homelands as they would be likely to be imprisoned, or worse, for having joined a foreign army. The Queen urged that they should be treated honourably, and a scheme was set up offering them the opportunity to go to the Cape or other British colonies. Led by their commander at Shorncliffe, Major-General Baron Von Stutterheim, over two thousand five hundred men went to South Africa where they were given land and a wage on the understanding that they would serve with British forces to protect

Marriage Certificate of Sergeant Manduka. At Cheriton Church on the 31st March 1856, the Legionnaire Manduka married Mary Whitehead from Sandgate.

British interests there. Some, like Wladislav Manduka, chose to seek their fortunes in America. He was a mercenary from Poland and, upon joining the BGL, was immediately appointed a sergeant in the 2nd Light Dragoons at Shorncliffe. It has been suggested that girls from the local workhouse were 'made available' to the Legionnaires. What is certain is that, like many of his comrades, Manduka married a local girl, and his wedding to Mary Whitehead of Sandgate took place at Cheriton parish church on the 31st March 1856. After his discharge from the BGL the couple went to America where he joined the New York 25th Cavalry and fought in the American Civil War. He deserted Mary and took a second and even a third 'wife' and died in Baltimore in 1897, being buried in Loudon Park National Military Cemetery. There then followed a dispute between Mary and Manduka's second 'wife' over who was entitled to his pension. Finding in favour of Mary, the pensions officer described this colourful character as *"a scoundrel...a drinking man of bad reputation."*

Sandgate War Memorial. The plaque commemorating Queen Victoria's visit in 1855 is to the right of the memorial.

A century and a half after the Legionnaires left Shorncliffe there are no visible reminders of their presence in the area; no statues or memorials, no road or inn names as a reminder of this unique period in the area's history. At the lower end of Military Road in Sandgate, near the War Memorial, there is set in the wall a plaque

QUEEN ELIZABETH
RESTED AT SANDGATE CASTLE
25TH AUGUST 1575
AND
QUEEN VICTORIA
WITH THE PRINCE CONSORT
VISITED SANDGATE
ON THEIR WAY TO SHORNCLIFFE CAMP
9TH AUGUST 1855

The Plaque. A close up view of the plaque. This is the only memorial to the 5000 men of the British German Legion. It also records the visit of Queen Elizabeth I nearly 300 years earlier.

commemorating the visit of Queen Victoria on the 9th August 1855. It mentions her visit to Shorncliffe camp but, alas, makes no mention of the foreign troops whom she had come to review. However, some of the soldiers stayed in the local area and became integrated into the community; a number of local businesses especially shops, hotels and guest houses being run by Legionnaires and their descendants. A book published just after the Great War described how Folkestone had been 'Germanicised' in the 1850s *"when German troops were lent to fight the Russian Bear." The book continues, "The soldiers were profitable to Folkestone. When they were dispersed or demobilised, they left a certain number in the town. They married and multiplied and took some part in governing the simple natured of Folkestone who were originally smugglers and fishermen."* This somewhat harsh judgment by John Jones on the indigenous population of Folkestone no doubt has some truth. With the outbreak of the Great War, most of the descendants of the German Legionnaires were rounded up as enemy aliens and sent off to internment camps; it is not known how many may have returned after the war nor how many local residents might today be able to trace their ancestry back to a soldier from the British German Legion.

Chapter 6

THE HYTHE STAFF BARRACKS AND THE SCHOOL OF MUSKETRY

Since the end of the Napoleonic Wars, when Hythe had been literally overwhelmed by the military presence, there had been a steady exodus of soldiers. The description of Hythe by W.H. Ireland in his *History of the County of Kent,* published in 1828, paints a picture of the town before the effects of this decline had made its impact,

> Hythe has a neat little theatre, some good and spacious inns, a subscription reading room and an excellent public library. The shops as well as the dwellings belonging to the superior classes of inhabitants, speak of the opulence, respectability and commercial importance of the place. There are many pleasant houses upon the ledges of the cliff above the town, commanding delightful and extensive views both of the sea and neighbouring country, as well as numerous convenient habitations appropriated for the use of strangers during the bathing season. Others are occupied by the families of officers of rank in the army stationed in this place, who greatly contribute to, enliven and improve the society constantly frequenting the town of Hythe.

Ireland was not to know that, within a few years, the Staff Barracks would be quit by the Royal Staff Corps, the barracks on the hills of Saltwood demolished and that the 'neat little theatre' would close its doors for the last time in 1837. Whilst it is true that Hythe lamented the loss of the military, it did not suffer to the same extent as Folkestone. The town was

Hythe 1850. This watercolour by 'RW' is called 'The School of Infantry, Hythe'. Note the redcoats practising drill. Beyond them, the building is probably Fort Sutherland. The monument to the right has not been identified.

sufficiently well established as a fashionable resort to continue to attract visitors, and the Corporation did well to maintain the town's popularity. In 1854, for instance, a bathing establishment was built at a cost of £2000 incorporating a domed roof, rest rooms and living accommodation for a guide. But the turning point was in 1853 when the army returned to the town in the form of the newly created Corps of Instructors in Musketry. The elite rifle regiments already had their own systems of training but, in 1852, Lord Hardinge, the Commander in Chief, had decided that a national system of training was needed, with regimental officers and NCOs being trained at a central school, and taking their skills back to their regiments. The new school made its headquarters in the Staff Barracks, and the old Waggon Train barracks on the opposite side of the canal were demolished and turned into a parade ground. The extensive shingle beaches nearby were ideally suited to target practice and ranging. The School of Musketry had arrived in Hythe and would remain in the town for over a hundred years.

The School of Musketry, Hythe. An unusual view of the School, with the trees and buildings covered in snow.

It is curious that the School of Musketry should have been so named; during the era of the musket, a weapon that relied on firing mass volleys rather than accuracy, there was little need for the specialist instruction offered by the School. It was with the general introduction of the rifle that the job of arms instruction was taken out of the hands of the drill sergeant and placed with trained instructors. Since its introduction in 1800, the British Army had gradually introduced the Baker Rifle, but it was a slow process. Although a great improvement in terms of range and accuracy over the Brown Bess musket, it was a cumbersome weapon and actually took longer than the musket to load. Then, in 1849, a Frenchman named Minie invented a rifle where the bullets did not have to be rammed laboriously down the barrel, but where they expanded on firing and spun neatly through the rifling of the barrel. With its range of 1000 yards compared to the 200 yards of the Baker rifle, the Minie was a far superior weapon. It was unfortunate that, although the British army started to re-equip in 1851, the process was so slow that the Brown Bess musket remained the mainstay of the Line regiments all through the Crimean War[11].

The School opened in June 1853 under the command of Lieutenant-Colonel Charles Crawford Hay of the 19th Regiment, the Green Howards. With him, Colonel Hay brought two other members of his regiment; Lieutenant Currie to act as adjutant and Colour Sergeant John M'Kay. Three sergeant instructors, Giles Ruston, 3rd Battalion Grenadier Guards, William Lobes, 2nd Battalion Grenadier Guards and George Morris of the 97th Regiment soon arrived and, on the 7th

[11] See Appendix F, 'A Short History of Small Arms'

Musketry instructor. This Sergeant-Major of Musketry of 1853 is holding a Minie rifle.

August, 1853, the School was opened under the name Corps of Instructors in Musketry and was ready to receive its first intake. The art of shooting, hitherto often as dangerous to the firer as to the fired upon, now became a science. The official opening of the School took place in 1854 when it received its Royal Warrant. During his time at the school Hay laid down the principles of modern rifle shooting. He rapidly rose to the rank of General and his introductory address to new students included the proposition that 2000 men who could shoot were better than 200,000 who could not. He was a fair shot himself, but his talent for hitting his own (admittedly enlarged) target on the beach from St. Leonards churchyard, a mile away, was no doubt unsettling for some of the residents of Hythe.

Courses would last for between six and seven weeks and, for some reason now lost in the mists of time, were called 'Parties', with each party being divided into a 'Left Wing' and a 'Right Wing'. Officers and NCOs had separate courses and, indeed, separate quarters. The course developed a reputation for being tough and by the turn of the 20th century the student's day started at 8.15 am finished at 4.30 pm with night firing exercises and a good hour's homework to be done. In 1915 one student wrote on a postcard home, *"One day gone and still alive. My word – work – I didn't know what it was till I came here and the worst of it is that it gets worse and worse."* Little wonder that those who passed out with a First Class certificate from Hythe were proud of the fact. The soldier of 30 years earlier had a somewhat more relaxed time; work commencing at 9.30 am and finishing at 2.30 pm.

For some students, particularly of the Wellingtonian era, the course was simply too challenging; John Fisher was 20 years old when the Royal Navy sent him to Hythe and his journal provides an amusing and irreverent account of his course,

In 1861, when I was sent to Hythe School of Musketry as a young Lieutenant, I found myself in a small squad of

School Instructors and Staff 1860. A rare early photograph. The school clock is now displayed at Hythe Library and Museum.

officers. My right hand man was a General and my left hand man a full Colonel. The Colonel spent his time drawing pictures of the General. (The Colonel was really a wonderful artist). The General was splendid. He was a magnificent man with a voice like a bull and his sole object was Mutiny! He hated General Hay, who was in command of the Hythe School of Musketry. He hated him with a contemptuous disdain.

In those days we commenced firing at a target only a few hundred yards off. The General never hit the target once! The Colonel made a beautiful picture of him addressing the Parade and General Hay: "Gentlemen! My unalterable conviction is that the bayonet is the true weapon of the British soldier!" The beauty of the situation was that the General had been sent to Hythe to qualify as Inspector General of Musketry.

This was not the end of the General's mutinous behaviour, as Fisher explains,

> After some weeks of careful drill (without firing a shot) we had to snap caps (that was to get our nerves all right I suppose!): the Sergeant Instructor walked along the front of the squad and counted ten copper caps into each outstretched hand. At that critical moment, General Hay appeared on the Parade. This gave the General his chance! With his bull-like voice he asked General Hay if it was believable after those weeks of incessant application that we were going (each of us) to be entrusted with ten copper caps!
>
> When we were examined viva voce we each had to stand up to answer a question (like the little boys at Sunday School). The General was asked to explain the lock of the latest type of British Rifle. He got up and stated that as he was neither Maskelyne and Cooke nor the Davenport Brothers (who were the greatest conjurors at the time) he couldn't do it. Certainly we had some appalling questions. One that I had was "what do you pour the water into the barrel of the rifle with when you are cleaning it?" I said, "With a tin pannikin or the palm of the hand." The right answer was, "With care!"
>
> All the same I had a lovely time there; the British army was very kind to me and I loved it. The best shot in the

British Army at that time was a confirmed drunkard who trembled like a leaf, but when he got his eye on the target he was a bit of marble and 'bull's eyes' every time.

As well as clearly enjoying his time at Hythe, Fisher learned a great deal. He went on to the Navy's own gunnery school at HMS Excellent where he gained a reputation for innovation, especially in torpedo tactics. He is credited with the development of the big gun battleships, HMS Dreadnought and her sisters and, with the outbreak of war in 1914, as Lord Fisher of Keddlestone, he was appointed as First Sea Lord.

That there was humour, as well as hard work, to be found at Hythe is not surprising. One student, Lieutenant J.C. Robinson of the 30th Regiment, found time to record his observations in a sketch book, and these were reproduced in The Graphic of 23rd April 1881, with the following amusing storyline:

In these sketches we have a humorous view of student life at the well-known School of Musketry at Hythe. The 'course' lasts two months, and on the first day the distribution of arms for use during that period is effected. Short carbines are served out to the officers of mounted regiments and long Martini Henry rifles to those in the Infantry branch of the service, and the effect is somewhat ludicrous when the cavalry officer happens to be abnormally tall and the Infantry officer rather under than over the middle height. Our next sketch shows the difficulty experienced by a student who is not quite so young or so lissom as he used to be, and who consequently fails to 'get well down on the heel'. He, however, manages to secure the requisite degree of steadiness by using a couple of 'Red Books' in

Musketry Sketches. Drawn by Lieutenant Robinson in 1881 to illustrate his description of a course of Musketry at Hythe.

Hard Work! This card show the metamorphosis endured by the student during his course at Hythe.

the manner shown in the following sketch. In 'Volley Firing' the anxiety of the instructor that the whole squad should fire precisely at the same moment is indicated by their gestures and simultaneous comments and entreaties. The 'Pet shot' is always the subject of absorbing interest and obsequious attention. A blanket is held up to protect him from the wind. One instructor carefully directs his position and another scans the target through a field glass to note the exact effect of his shot, whilst the remainder of the squad await the result with breathless interest and admiration. A hard morning's work in the open air sharpens the appetite amazingly, but for all that the late arrivals at the mess room cannot help feeling some degree of disappointment as they see the last fragrant pie rapidly disappearing, and nothing but cold meat left to fall back on. Their only consolation must be that the heavy feeders alone will suffer from the 'Student's nightmare', depicted in the next sketch. On his breast sits a strange monster, half cartridge, half instructor, armed with the model rifles from the lecture room, with wires attached to show the line of fire and trajectory, which the spectre seems to be driving into his brain, whilst on his cheeks he feels the hot sulphurous breath of a creeping monster in the shape of a rifle, and the target endowed with life and boxing gloves, dares him to hit it now. At last comes

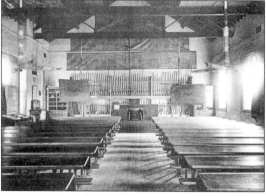

The Lecture Room. Note the racks of rifles and muskets at the front of the room.

the final examination, and the solemn moment when the confidential report is sealed up, each student being troubled with misgivings as to the verdict so far as it concerns himself, a condition of mind which, however, quietly gives place to one of exuberant joy, as he reflects that his course is done, and that he need no longer pore over the musketry regulations.

The men who managed to secure a place on a summer party at Hythe might just find time to enjoy the canal and a stroll down Ladies Walk, but a course during the winter months could involve a cold and wet day in the butts. The following description, from The Illustrated London News of the 18th February 1860, would have prompted the cautious student to pack extra warm clothing,

For those who love gunnery there is nothing more pleasant than a trip to Hythe, albeit a more desolate seaside place can scarcely be seen. The town nestles snugly enough under a range of hills...but the beach has a most bankrupt dreary air, with a set of baths (shut up), one row of lodging houses and a large, half finished shell of another. It bristles at intervals, as far as the eye can reach, with Martello towers, where the volunteers are exercised, and from which danger flags are waived to the mariners when practice commences in the butts. The musketry ground is a long, deep shingle, fearfully trying to walkers who are not quite up to the mark, and about half a mile broad. It is sadly windy, and, as they are obliged to shoot towards the sea, there is no suitable background for the eye; but still, many first class shots are trained there. The eighteen foot target of General Hay, the Commandant, is a very prominent object, and on each side of it are ranged the targets for the men, with little cast iron huts, from which the effect of the shots is telegraphed by means of different flags, held in different positions.

The reference to shingle in this item from The Illustrated London News is a reminder of a fact often

Range Practice. An early engraving demonstrating firing in the kneeling and standing positions. Martello Towers in the background.

overlooked. The School moved into the old Staff Barracks, but the practice of musket shooting required plenty of safe open space. As far back as 1812, land had been acquired by the Board of Ordnance on the Hythe foreshore for military training but, at only 26 acres, it was not nearly enough to cater for the needs of the new School. Accordingly, in 1853, a further 218 acres of beach and hinterland were purchased and it is here, on what became Shorncliffe Ranges and Hythe Ranges, that the main training in target and ranging practice took place

Although the principal role of the School was the study and instruction in the use of small arms, there was a secondary role; to ensure that the weapons issued to the army were tried and tested and were the best available. Hythe, in effect, became a weapons testing station. Not all recommendations, however, were received by the mandarins of Whitehall with enthusiasm. Despite Lieutenant-Colonel McMahon, chief instructor at the School in 1905-9, producing a positive report on the use of the machine-gun it was dismissed as a weapon to be used only against "savages and non-Christians." The Germans, on the other hand, snapped up the idea. The School was also at the forefront of the development of target technology. From simple beginnings of linen stretched over a wooden frame, to mechanical then electrical pop-up and moving targets, the School provided the most innovative challenges for its students. One 19th century officer recorded,

> On Monday we fired ten rounds file firing, ten rounds volley firing and ten rounds skirmishing. The last is beautiful work. We loaded as we ran, and fired at distances, and we were kept advancing and retiring as much as possible, so as to confuse us.

During its 116 years the School of Musketry, later renamed as the Small Arms and Signals Wing of the School of Infantry, taught thousands of men. Most infantry officers and NCOs passed through the School at some time in their career,

Officers' Course 1900. Course photograph of the 193rd Party. A fine display of moustaches!

sometimes joined by students from Ghana, Singapore, Jamaica, Guyana and Zambia. Even officers of the British German Legion were sent there for training during their time at Shorncliffe and, during the First World War, the School remained open and provided instruction for those destined for the Western

Front, including many Canadians. Looking at the lists of students of the School over the years, many names are familiar; men who were or went on to become famous. It would be an impossible task to list them all; we shall settle for just two examples. In January 1879 the 13th Hussars sent 20 year old sub-lieutenant Robert Baden-Powell, who was home from India on doctor's orders, on the Hythe course. At this time, the British army was fighting the Zulu Wars and, as Baden-Powell was applying himself to his studies, Colour Sergeant Frank Bourne of the 24th Regiment, was defending Rorke's Drift. Bourne did not receive a Victoria Cross for his part in the action; instead he accepted a commission and the appointment, in 1893, as Adjutant at Hythe School of Musketry. Meanwhile, Baden-Powell went on to win fame in the Boer Wars and as founder of the Scout movement. He died in Kenya in 1941 at the age of 83, whilst Bourne went on to outlive all of the other Rorke's Drift defenders, and died as a Lieutenant-Colonel on VE Day, the 8th May, 1945, at the age of 91.

In 1915 the School took on an additional responsibility; that of training aircraft machine gunners for the Royal Flying Corps. The Machine Gun School, later the School of Aerial Gunnery, operated from an aerodrome built on land at Palmarsh, close to the Dymchurch Redoubt, but it was Company Quartermaster Sergeant Chaney from the School of Musketry who organised the training. So dedicated was he that it was said that he could often be seen strapped to the wing of an aircraft experimenting with new techniques, such as synchronising the gun to fire through the blades of a moving propeller. To help train and assess pilots and air gunners, camera guns had been developed at the beginning of the war. One of the best known of these devices, made by Thornton Pickard of Altrincham, was the Hythe Camera Gun Mark III. It was similar in weight and shape to a Lewis gun and took still exposures on a 120mm film. The officers attending the Machine Gun School were billeted at the Hotel Imperial and took full advantage of the hotel's golf course; this had to be carefully arranged as the RFC gunners also used the golf links to practice firing against ground targets!

The Hotel Imperial, Hythe, as it was just before the Great War.

Wilbert Gilroy had first visited the Hotel Imperial in July 1915 and was to remember its charm when he returned to Hythe in 1917 for his aerial gunnery training. Gilroy did not start the war as a pilot; he had enlisted in Canada in 1914 as a qualified dentist and arrived at Shorncliffe in 1915, destined to spend the war years caring for the teeth of the Canadian troops. In a letter to his mother dated July 4th

The Flying Dentist. Wilbert Gilroy from Canada started the war as a dentist, but finished as a pilot in the RFC. He received his aerial gunnery training at Hythe.

1915, written on hotel notepaper, Gilroy explains, *"...my two chums and myself walked down to Hythe, which is about 1¹/₄ miles from the camp. There is a lovely beach here so we lay on the sand and sleep or talk. This afternoon it was so nice we went in for a paddle, up to our knees. It was grand on the beach, then at 7.30pm we had dinner at this hotel, which is a typical English hotel of the better class."* But the security of life as a battalion dentist was not Gilroy's destiny; he wanted to be in the air, as perhaps was presaged in another letter home in the summer of 1915, *"We had rather a pleasant surprise yesterday afternoon, one of the big British aircraft, which had been patrolling the Channel all morning in search of a German submarine, came over our camp. It was one of the Astra Torres type, like a Zeppelin, only just half the size, being 250 feet long while the zeps are 500 ft. It came right over our tent just about 100 feet from ground and we could see the thing very distinctly. Beneath the huge envelope was an armoured effect. This had portholes just like a boat and we could see the men's heads sticking out of them. They hollered down to us and we had the band play the National Anthem for them. We see dozens of aircraft but this is the closest yet. I was glad it wasn't a German."*

Gilroy began to pester the authorities to be allowed to transfer to the Royal Flying Corps and flight training and, in 1916, he was rewarded for his persistence. After qualifying as a pilot he returned to Hythe in January 1917 to take the course in aerial gunnery and found himself once again at the Hotel Imperial. Wilbert Gilroy was posted to the Western Front where he flew many sorties until, in October 1917, he was caught alone by three German fighters. With his own gun jammed all he could do was to try and evade the enemy. His plane was hit several times but he managed to lose his pursuers and land safely, despite also taking a bullet in the leg. This was the end of Gilroy's flying career, but he survived the war and returned to Canada where he resumed his dental practice.

It was a bitter blow to Hythe when the Small Arms School left the town in 1968. The town and the School had formed a very real attachment to each other and had come through two world wars and many other conflicts together. The familiar sights of uniformed Officers and NCOs marching through the town to Church Parade on Sunday mornings, strolling down Ladies Walk and

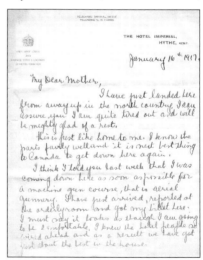

A Letter Home. The letter written by Gillroy to his mother on Hotel Imperial notepaper. The Imperial was used as officer's accommodation by those attending the aerial gunnery school.

rowing on the canal became just memories. At the turn of the twentieth century the uniform of the British Army too had been standardised, with a preponderance of khaki, broken by occasional splashes of blue and tartan, but the church parades of earlier days must have been altogether more spectacular. Writing in 1892, W.S. Miller describes such an occasion,

> The Church parade presents a brilliant spectacle — Life Guards, Blues, Dragoons, Lancers, Hussars, Guardsmen, Highlanders, Riflemen, Fusiliers, Royal Marines, militia men and Volunteers, with a sprinkling from the West India Regiments, and Lagos Constabulary combine to form a picture which for variety of uniform, and brilliancy of colour is quite unique.

The loss of the troops also had an impact on the commercial heart of the town. To quench the military thirst there had been a steady rise in the number of inns and taverns so that, by 1887, there were no less than twenty within a stone's throw of Red Lion Square. Just 100 years later only nine remained open. One of the public houses which has survived is the Hope Inn in Stade Street

NCO's Course 1907. The uniforms worn by these students on the 251st Party must have made a colourful spectacle.

which has its own military history. At the time of the construction of the Royal Military Canal, the men of the Royal Waggon Train had their canteen on the premises, with officers' quarters, stables and a hospital occupying surrounding buildings. The army moved out in 1827 when the premises acquired a liquor licence, and was then named after Colonel Hope who had assisted William Pitt in selecting sites for the south coast Martello Towers.

With the closure of the School there was also a question mark over the future of the Ranges; would they be closed and the land sold to developers? By 1969, despite the best efforts of a skeleton staff of civilians, the Ranges were deserted and becoming derelict. However, a combination of creative thinking by the recently retired Major Dougie Maber, and the intervention of Mother Nature, brought a new lease of life to the facilities and secured their future. Appointed to the civilian role of Range Officer after his retirement, Maber scouted round to find potential users

Officers' Mess dining room. The nearest portrait is of Major-General Crawford Hay, the first commandant of the School.

for the Ranges and soon there was interest from various Territorial units in the south east, the Police, as well as the Marines from Deal and local gun clubs. All thought of developing the site perished when a trial bore hole discovered that, underneath the shingle, there existed a water table with 'an obnoxious fluid content'. The Ranges have gone from strength to strength and, together with Lydd Ranges, make up the Cinque Ports Training Area, where they continue to offer general and specialist weapons training for the British army. Dougie Maber died in November 2000.

Of the Staff Barracks, later the School of Musketry, little remains. The main buildings were demolished in the 1960s and replaced by a modern office complex. At first sight the only links with the past are a few road names; Barrack Hill, Military Road, Twiss Road, and the newer streets of Sir John Moore Avenue and Corunna Close. But there are some more substantial reminders of the past; fronting Military Road is Military Terrace, a row of half a dozen homes that may have originally been occupied by civilian workers at the Staff Barracks. A walk round Sir John Moore Avenue reveals that two more buildings survived the developer's attentions. On the north side of the road is

Hythe High Street c1915. The School remained open during the Great War. These soldiers are returning to Shorncliffe camp after a day's training at the School.

an impressive red brick building dated 1893, clearly an addition to the School of Musketry. More importantly, on the opposite side of the road stands Hay House, named after Lieutenant-Colonel Charles Crawford Hay, the first commandant of the School of Musketry. But the house is, in fact, that purchased in 1809 for occupation by Colonel John Brown of the Royal Staff Corps when he was supervising the building of the Royal Military Canal. Both buildings are private homes and can only be viewed externally. But there is one final feature that provides an even more poignant link with the past and to appreciate it we are going to return to Rifleman Harris of the 95th Rifles[12]. Having survived Corunna, Harris and the remnants of his regiment returned to Hythe barracks to recover and recruit replacements. In July 1809 the regiment undertook the day's march from Hythe to Deal to embark upon the ill-fated Walcheren Expedition. The object of the enterprise was to attack the harbours in Holland where Napoleon was rebuilding his

fleet after its destruction at Trafalgar. No sooner had the troops landed than they began to fall ill. The illness spread like wildfire and, by the end of August, so many men had succumbed that the attack was no longer viable, the operation was terminated and the survivors were embarked and brought home. The 95th, together with the 43rd and 52nd eventually made it back to Hythe. Harris describes the scene: *"So filled with sick was the hospital at Hythe, that the barracks also became a hospital. As deaths ensued and thinned the wards, the men were continually removed, progressing from barrack to hospital, and from hospital to the grave."* What we now know is that the men were afflicted with malaria. The question is where were they buried? Nearly two hundred men of the 95th died during this period, together with many from other regiments, but all that can be accounted for are 76 who

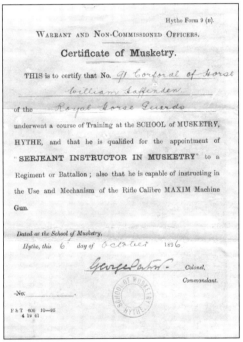

The Prize! The coveted Certificate in Musketry from Hythe. This one was awarded to Corporal of Horse William Haffenden of the Royal Horse Guards in 1896.

were buried at Saltwood church. There has been speculation that the rest might have been buried at St Leonard's in Hythe, but that cannot have been the case; St Leonard's was too far away from the the Staff Barracks or those on Barrack Hill, and there are no records of these men having been buried there. The impression given by Harris is of a burial place much nearer to the barracks. The answer may be in a sandstone slab found built into the wall of an old ball alley, discovered by Colonel Slade, who was Commandant at Hythe in between 1890 and 1894. The slab was

[12] See Chapter 2.

etched with the Bugle Horn emblem and was inscribed: '*95th Regt, 2nd Bat, 1811*'. It also bore the name '*Lt Col. H. Wade*'. This alley was a part of the barracks which was built on the site of the graveyard of St. Nicholas' Church. The church itself was destroyed in about 1700 but the graveyard remained and is clearly shown on Ordnance Survey and other maps of the area to the present day. Add to this the fact that the Kent Archaeological Rescue Unit found skeletal remains on the site in the early twentieth century and also during a dig in 1978, and it therefore seems likely that Rifleman Harris' comrades were buried here. Could it be that Colonel Wade, who had commanded the 2nd Battalion of the 95th on the Walcheren Expedition in 1809, had erected the memorial stone where many of his men were buried and that when the burial site was built over the stone was salvaged and placed in the wall of the ball alley? Much of the site of St. Nicholas' graveyard now lies under the houses and bungalows of Corunna Close, but there remains an open area of land on which grows a tangle of shrubbery beneath which can just be seen large pieces of stone, perhaps from the old church itself and, maybe, the remains of soldiers of the 95th still lie here, in the spot where they were buried so hastily nearly 200 years ago.

Chapter 7

THE VICTORIAN ERA

With the dawn of the Victorian era, and especially the arrival of the railway in 1843, Folkestone began to cast off its mantle of simplicity. The Victorians, for whom the 'seaside' was to become a national institution, discovered the town and the population, only 4,000 in the 1840s, rapidly increased. There was an explosion in the building of

houses, hotels and other amenities. Folkestone became fashionable and soon challenged Hythe as the playground of the well-to-do. One of the first of many notable Victorians to make use of the new rail service to Folkestone was Charles Dickens; over the next two decades he was a regular visitor and his descriptions of the town as it emerged from obscurity to its place as a rival of Brighton and the Wells are worth recalling:

Folkestone 1857. Looking towards Folkestone from the Canterbury Road, this engraving shows the town dominated by Cubitt's railway viaduct.

> …you used to be dropped upon the platform of the main line at eleven o'clock on a dark winter's night, in a roaring wind; and in the howling wilderness outside the station was a short omnibus, which brought you up by the forehead the instant that you got in the door; and nobody cared about you, and you were alone in the world. You bumped over infinite chalk, until you were turned out at a strange building which had just left off being a barn without having quite begun to be a house, where nobody expected you coming, or knew what to do with you when you were come, and where you were usually blown about, until you happened to be blown against the cold beef, and finally into bed.

These were clearly the very early days when the South Eastern Railway Company had hastily hired a Folkestone boat-builder's shed as a refuge and refreshment stop for its clientele, many of whom were to experience even greater

Folkestone 1844. A sketch by Henry Moses showing the gas works, the Pavilion Hotel and the Custom House. It is also possible to make out the Slope Road which, today, is the Road of Remembrance. (WD)

discomfort on the cross channel steamer to Boulogne. If Folkestone was to prosper, improvements clearly had to be made. It was Jacob, Earl of Radnor, who rose to the challenge and, in 1845, engaged the London architect, Sydney Smirke, to develop his Folkestone Estate. Smirke published a prospectus extolling the virtues of the town,

> The genius of Steam, that has already effected so many extraordinary social changes in this country, has been peculiarly active here. A few years ago this small secluded town lay unfrequented and little known...We find it now with a Railway direct from London, a capacious harbour for large ships, a fine stone pier, and an Hotel with hundreds of beds...
>
> This change in character of Folkestone has been so wonderfully rapid, that we find it now almost without a house to receive a visitor.
>
> A plan is laid down for the proposed arrangement of the building sites: their general aspect will be varied and irregular: it is intended specially to avoid the dull straight uniformity of most of our watering places: there will be no cheerless crowding together of close tenements, but plenty of air and space, and uninterrupted sea views will be preserved everywhere.

After several abortive schemes, in 1849 Smirke eventually produced a plan that saw the development of Sandgate Road, the Leas and its Promenade and the West Cliff Estate, which remain the most attractive features of the town today. Smirke also mentions the capacious hotel,

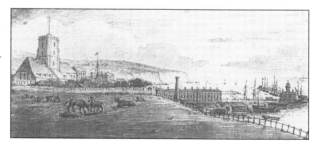

Folkestone Harbour 1844. Another drawing by Henry Moses, this time by moonlight. (WD)

undoubtedly the Pavilion Hotel down by the harbour. Dickens (who for some reason referred to Folkestone as Pavilionstone) was delighted with the hotel and sang its praise,

If you are going to our Great Pavilionstone Hotel, the sprightliest of porters under the sun, whose cheerful looks are a pleasant welcome, shoulder your luggage, drive it off in vans, bowl it away in trucks, and enjoy themselves in playing athletic games with it...you walk into that establishment as if it were your club; and find ready for you, your news room, dining room, smoking room, billiard room, music room, public breakfast, public dinner twice a day (one plain, one gorgeous), hot baths and cold baths.

A thoroughly good inn, in the days of coaching and posting, was noble place. But no such inn would have been equal to the reception of four or five hundred people, all of them wet through, and half of them dead sick, every day of the year.

It is upon such recommendation that Folkestone soon acquired a reputation for good service and respectable society and, at a time of optimism spurred by the new wealth created by the industrial revolution, Sydney Smirke's call to investors was well timed. However, the reference in his prospectus to crowded tenements hinted at the truth that, for the majority of the population, the reality of life was poverty and squalor. As the century progressed a social conscience began to awaken and so did the pace of social reform.

The lot of the common soldier at this time was no better than that of the agricultural labourer or urban worker. During the wars with the French, the army had bathed in glory at home as laurel-wreathed coaches cantered through village and town bearing news of Salamanca, Vittoria and Waterloo. With peace declared, and many

Shorncliffe Camp from Sandgate. This view etched in the 1850s does not do justice to the steep hill from the village to the camp.

officers returning to their estates on half pay, the army was looked upon again with suspicion and as an unnecessary expense. Soldiers remained in barracks, rarely to be seen in public. That is not to say that the great and the good were slow to show their appreciation to the defenders of the Empire. For example, as British troops from the Crimea returned to Shorncliffe in September 1856, to the huts recently vacated by the British German Legion, a special welcome was laid on for them by local dignitaries and businessmen. The event was reported in the local newspaper.

Crimean Dinner At Folkestone

The people of Folkestone gave an interesting entertainment on Tuesday last. The medal men of the 6th Inniskilling Dragoons, 11th Hussars, E Troop Royal Artillery, Hythe School of Musketry and Coast Guard, were invited to a substantial feast in a large tent erected in the grounds of the Pavilion Hotel, Folkestone which Mr. Breach, the proprietor, had kindly offered for the occasion. Mr. Hoad of Folkestone, assisted by the South Eastern Railway Company, had erected a tent capable of holding 800 persons which was decorated with the flags of all nations and with laurels and other evergreens combining agreeably with the gay colours of the soldiers' uniforms. The dinner which consisted of roast beef, game pies, lamb, mutton, and plum pudding, was assisted down by plenty of beer, ale and rum punch after which each soldier received a quantity of cigars and tobacco.

Private De Carte, on returning thanks on behalf of his fellow soldiers said, "We lost many a brave man, but we never lost our good name or honour. We cannot forget Miss Florence Nightingale, nor can we forget mismanagement (cheers and laughter). I promised if I ever returned, I would drink to the ladies who so nobly risked their lives for us – let us do so now."

The health of Miss Nightingale was then drunk amidst enthusiastic cheers, and the company separated.

Whilst the men were no doubt pleased to be back on English soil after the privations of the Crimea, Shorncliffe barracks were by no means perfect. In a report to the Barrack and Hospitals Improvement Commission in October, 1858, praise for the healthiness of Shorncliffe was tempered by noting that the water supply was sufficient only for drinking and washing, with little to spare for sanitation. The camp consisted of 192 wooden huts, each for 25 men, but there were only 80 married quarters. The report condemned the fact that six families would have to occupy a single hut in *"conditions both indecent and unhealthy."* There were no baths anywhere on the camp and the oil lighting was totally inadequate. The Royal Artillery barracks, built during the Napoleonic wars, were condemned because of their primitive sanitary arrangements that were worse than those in the wooden huts. The small hospital, also a wooden structure, had no accommodation for families; babies were delivered in a small house some distance from the camp.

Despite the report, Shorncliffe was a popular camp with the soldiers. It may be that it was because the report's authors were friends of Florence Nightingale that

stop at the Imperial Hotel with *"the most recent appliances for securing that luxurious comfort, which enters so largely into modern life and manners,"* might tempt the visitor to venture no further. Built in 1880 on the site of the derelict Twiss Fort, the hotel was the last word in Victorian splendour, and had cost £30,000. The following year had witnessed the

Hythe to Sandgate Tram. This unique photo from c1910 shows the tram about to leave Sandgate. The roof could be removed, giving rise to the nickname 'the toastrack'.

spectacular opening of Princes Parade by the Prince of Wales. Once the tram arrived in Sandgate a few steps walk offered the choice of recuperation at either the Royal Norfolk Hotel or the Royal Kent Hotel after which the intrepid traveller could take a lift up the cliff to the Leas. Progress into the town centre might here be interrupted by afternoon tea at the Grand or Metropole, the twin edifices of Victorian grandeur. With further halts to enjoy the music, often provided by a military band, at one of the three bandstands along the cliff top walk, the journey from Folkestone to Hythe and back could easily consume the entire day.

Opening of Princes Parade, Seabrook, 1881. From The Illustrated London News. The Seabrook Hotel, later the Hotel Imperial, had been opened only the year before.

The military band has always been one of the most popular contributions that the army makes to town life. The Illuminated Garden Fete in August 1879 at the West Cliff Hotel in Folkestone would not have been nearly as enjoyable without the band of the 4th Hussars. After a day which threatened rain, the evening saw a clearing sky and, as dusk fell, the glow from festoons of Chinese Lanterns set off the flower beds and the bandstand. By 8pm there were several hundred guests gathered and they were entertained with a mixed programme of music by the Shorncliffe band; the most popular by far being a selection of "Reminiscences of Old England", including, *Home Sweet Home, Sally in Our Alley* and *Poor Tom Bowling*. During the intervals, the gardens were illuminated with coloured lights and *'fire balloons sent up in the air under the supervision of Messrs. Brock & Co the eminent pyrotechnists of Crystal Palace.'*

The horse was as common in the 19th century as the motor car is today, and with Dragoons and Hussars regularly stationed at Shorncliffe, regular race events were organised where local riders could pit their skills against the professional cavalrymen. Described as taking place on ground a few minutes walk of the Camp and Shorncliffe Station, one such was held in October 1897; it was a fine but cloudy day, ideal for horse racing and attracted a great many visitors. 'A commodious grandstand was erected, which was well patronised as were the refreshment tents of Mr Medhurst and Mr Ward of Sandgate. There were, of course, the usual amusements, Aunt Sally, roulette, shooting the nuts and swindles of all kinds'. There were eight races on the card including the Black Rock Stakes, the Borough Members Plate, the Canterbury

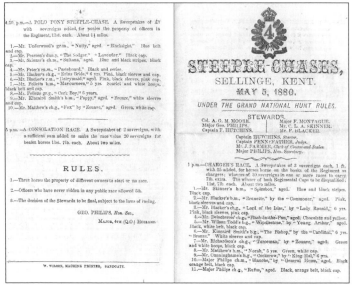

Racing Programme 1880. Races were a regular feature. This programme gives details of an event at Sellinge (sic) on the 5th May 1880 organised by the 4th Hussars, then stationed at Shorncliffe.

Cavalry Depot Stakes and the Shorncliffe Stakes, which was open only to horses owned by officers at Shorncliffe.

The horse could also be the harbinger of bad news; barely a week would pass without a story in the local newspapers reporting an accident or damage caused by a runaway horse. But the public would have been justified in expecting that army horses, at least, would not suffer from the unpredictable nature of their civilian cousins. A sad incident in February 1890 demonstrated that even the best trained cavalry horse could still be a danger in the hands of a drunken rider. It was 5 o'clock in the afternoon when four year-old Fred Sadler was returning home from Sandgate School with his seven year-old sister. Without warning, the children were trampled under the hooves of the horses ridden by two troopers of the 8th Hussars who had both been drinking. Whilst his sister suffered only minor injuries, poor little Fred was badly kicked leaving him with a fractured skull, from which he was not expected to recover. The following Saturday the troopers, Privates George Rob and Thomas Bell, appeared before the Folkestone Police Court charged with furious riding. Evidence was heard from a witness, the Reverend Woodward, who said he had seen the men galloping their horses in Sandgate. Rob endeavoured to rein his horse in, but Bell was urging his on. The reverend remembered seeing some children playing in the road and, on turning round, he saw one of the horses run over a little girl. Finding the two men guilty, the justice warned them that, if Fred did not survive, they would likely be charged with manslaughter. Rob was fined ten shillings, Bell twenty shillings with each being ordered to carry out 14 days hard labour if they failed to pay. It is believed that Fred did, in fact, survive there being no burial records or newspaper accounts of his death at that time.

In a century when Britain was almost permanently at war, protecting her interests in the far flung corners of Empire, troops were often either leaving for or returning from some foreign conflict. The practice of the well-intentioned of Folkestone welcoming troops home had become a tradition; on their return from Egypt in 1882, the 4th Dragoon Guards, the Royal Irish and the Royal Artillery were treated to a banquet in

Trooper of the 4th Hussars. This cabinet photo was taken in Folkestone in the 1880s.

Shorncliffe's gymnasium by the town's businessmen. Apart from such events, or when training in a beauty spot, the humble soldier was rarely seen in public and his life was almost monastic. This was in stark contrast to the elegant lifestyle of army officers, and it is this difference that lies at the root of the ambivalence sometimes displayed in the attitude of the local community, and the world in general, towards

17th Lancers at Shorncliffe. A coloured engraving showing a regimental tournament. The competitors wear face masks and use wooden swords. The winners receive a pay rise of from 2d to 4d per week for the following year, ensuring that each contest is hotly fought.

the common soldier. The dashing young officers, many of whom were titled, were always welcomed at local events. Until the 1870s commissions were obtained by purchase, and it was only the sons of the nobility who could afford the price. This had created an officer class for whom war was seen as a sporting enterprise and where the cut of a uniform was valued more highly than professional soldiering.

It is a sad fact that, on the very site where Sir John Moore had introduced his enlightened ideas for the treatment and training of troops, fifty years after the General's death the lash was still being applied. The Folkestone Chronicle reported with distaste on the corporal punishment of one man at Shorncliffe in September 1859,

One of those disgraceful scenes so degrading to a British soldier, and discreditable to a country that allows it, took place at the camp on Thursday. Driver John Wele of No 3 battery, Royal Artillery was tried by a district court martial on Monday for desertion from the Military Hospital Shorncliffe (where he was a patient).

The court sentenced him to receive 50 lashes, to be branded with the letter D and to 84 days imprisonment.

The first portion of the sentence with the abominable lash was carried into effect on Thursday morning in the presence of his comrades and fellow men drawn up in Artillery square to witness the brutal punishment; the man received the full complement and was taken down from the triangle and disgraced and most likely a worse man through life than he otherwise would have been from the brutality of a power that can sanction the use of an instrument of torture that nearly all England cries shame on the tyrannical slave holders of America for using.

Flogging was finally abolished in peacetime in 1868, although discipline remained severe, apparently designed to suppress character and initiative.

The barracks at Shorncliffe during most of Queen Victoria's reign were those wooden huts which had been so hastily erected for the British German Legion; the policy was one of 'make do and mend'. The soldiers, and sometimes their wives, were expected to live in overcrowded and indecent conditions. It is little wonder that the men, expected to live under such demoralising conditions, should indulge in drink and that fights would often erupt. One incident in 1875 ended in death for two soldiers, both bandsmen in the 82nd regiment. The reasons for his actions were never explained, but John Morgan on one Saturday evening in early March took a razor to his friend, Joseph Foulstone, and cut his throat. The reports of the case claimed that the two men were drunk, as was another soldier who was present throughout the attack, but who was so comatose that he was not aware of the attack taking place only inches from him. Foulstone sustained horrific wounds; his neck was cut from ear to ear, the wind pipe completely severed and the bones exposed. Incredibly, he staggered from his hut into the one adjoining where, despite trying to staunch the flow with his hands, he was seen to be bleeding copiously. Unable to talk he signalled for pen and paper and managed to write down, *"John Morgan done this just now"*. A doctor was summoned, but Foulstone was dead within twenty minutes. Morgan was arrested and placed for his own safety in Folkestone Police Station until Monday morning, from where he was taken before Hythe Quarter Sessions which committed him for trial to the Assizes then sitting in Maidstone. Despite his denials, the jury found Morgan guilty of murder; there was only one sentence, death by hanging. The condemned man was kept in the County Gaol for his final days, his only visitor being his father, himself an old soldier, to whom he gave some photographs of himself to be given to his comrades at Shorncliffe camp. As the final day approached, Morgan made a confession of his crime but still no explanation was forthcoming. On the 30th March 1875, as the rope was placed around his neck, the nineteen year-old uttered not a word and took the reason for the horrific attack with him to the grave.

Drinking and fighting were not the only distractions for the soldiers; some sought solace not in the bottle but in the arms of the opposite sex, as seen from a report of 1890:

> A Shocking State of Affairs
> A frightful state of immorality appears to prevail at Shorncliffe Camp. Women haunt the locality by the scores and the information given to the Board of Guardians was absolutely shocking. The Military Hospital is full and the infirmary at the workhouse is burdened with similar cases. The Guardians have instructed their clerk to apply to the Commandant to order the military police to prevent females from sleeping about the camp. If found wandering about the roads without visible means of support, the police will be instructed to apprehend them.

Whilst the troops at Shorncliffe camp were languishing in little more than slum conditions, Folkestone and its environs were enjoying booming prosperity during the late 1800s; this was the period when the large Victorian redbrick mansions and hotels were

Art Treasures Exhibition. Opened in 1886, but better known as the Pleasure Gardens Theatre.

being built; in 1886 the Art Treasures Exhibition[14] opened in a building styled on the Crystal Palace, with the Victoria Pier being unveiled the following year. Even the camp presented a public façade that intrigued and attracted the Victorian visitor, unaware perhaps of the conditions that the men endured. The Holiday Annual of 1893 records the delight of a family day out, ending with a climb from Sandgate to Shorncliffe,

> But the Camp – oh! The Camp. There was a fear that I should have three young 'soldiers' to bring home. Many

[14] Two years later the building was renamed the Pleasure Gardens Theatre.

an hour we spent watching the redcoats, bluecoats, whitecoats and anything that held a gun or a sword and to see the cavalry galloping to the tune of 'Bonnie Dundee' was the height of happiness. Many a rest we had in the gymnasium watching the drill or laughing at the clumsy attempts of some recruit to imitate his betters.

Not all Victorians, however, were blind to social conditions. Disraeli had written of two nations existing side by side but in ignorance of each other. Amongst the social reformers spawned at this time there were some who had their eye on the army. Dr J. Lane Notter writing in 1890 pointed out that the heaviest concentration of population in England was 196,000 people to the square mile, yet barrack regulations permitted an equivalent of a staggering 400,000 to the square mile. Notter highlighted the effects such overcrowding could have on the soil especially where dirty and overcrowded streets hemmed in the soldiers' quarters. His recommendations for sanitation, heating and cleaning became a blueprint for barrack improvements; what was needed now was the money to finance what was essentially a slum clearance programme.

The obstacle to financing the much needed improvements to army barracks was principally political. The lion's share of defence spending continued to be directed to the Navy whilst the Army continued to be seen as a necessary evil, but one that should not be encouraged by the creation of large training camps at home. The catalyst for change came when Lord Randolph Churchill resigned as Chancellor of the Exchequer in 1888 and set himself to challenge the government over economic

waste. He advocated a programme of barrack reconstruction and the cause was taken up by Edward Stanhope who, as Secretary of State, steered through Parliament the Barracks Act of 1890. Of the four million pounds allocated for barrack works, £170,000 was spent at Shorncliffe. Together with further allocations during the next few years, this enabled all of the wooden huts to be demolished and replaced in brick. Many of these 'new' buildings remain and a drive around the camp perimeter road today reveals the rows of barrack blocks built in 1899 and 1900 and which form Napier Barracks. Somerset Barracks, which had been built a couple of years before, were originally intended for use by the cavalry. By 1901 the programme of rebuilding was completed and the last of the

Victorian Folkestone. A montage of views of the town in the 1880s.

Crimean huts was demolished. Ironically, however, this surge of modernity was tempered by the building, in 1903, of a large hutted camp just to the north of Napier. Officially named Risborough Barracks, these timber walled huts became popularly known as 'Tin Town', due to their corrugated iron roofs. It was also during this period that the size of the camp was considerably extended to the west by the purchase of large areas of pastureland at St. Martin's Plain and Dibgate. The completion of the building works at Shorncliffe was crowned by the passing of a set of Bye-laws which marked the end of over one hundred years of free access to the camp by the general public. As the following extracts from these regulations show, the camp had in the past attracted some dubious characters:

NOTICE
SHORNCLIFFE CAMP

NOW NOTICE is hereby given that His Majesty's Secretary of State for War...intends to make the following Bye-laws, viz:-

1. It shall not be lawful for any costermonger, sherbet seller, ice cream hawker, pedlar, huckster, marine or other dealer, or rag and bone, base metal or bottle gatherer, or person engaged in similar traffic or occupation, unless he or she is in possession of a Pass...to intrude or enter land at Shorncliffe camp.

2. It shall not be lawful for any person unless in possession of a Pass to camp, bivouac or sleep out upon the said land.

3. It shall not be lawful for any night walkers or common prostitute to locate herself in, or trespass on, or resort to the said land for the purpose of prostitution.

Dated the 25th April 1903.

Shorncliffe & Sandgate Station c 1870. Opened in 1863, and moved to its present location in 1878. Today it is known as Folkestone West.

For the troops posted to Shorncliffe camp, the usual point of arrival was Shorncliffe railway station and the men could count on a warm welcome from the locals. In November 1895, the 3rd Dragoons arrived at the station on their final leg of a journey back from India, and were greeted by a large crowd gathered on the platform and outside. The 400 men then marched through Cheriton to the camp. When they reached the White Lion in Cheriton they were met by the band of the King's Royal Rifles who played them back to their new home. That the band was at the White Lion rather than at the station to meet their comrades was not dwelt upon!

Although the railway had arrived in Folkestone in 1843, the original Shorncliffe & Sandgate station was not opened until 1863. It was renamed Shorncliffe Camp in 1874, the same year that the branch line through Hythe to Sandgate was opened. An underpass was built in 1878 and the whole station was rebuilt some 150 yards west of the early station in 1881 (It is this station which, in 1964, became Folkestone West). Not only was Shorncliffe a staging post for the troops; the bulk of the military supplies for the camp also arrived there. During the early 1880s the annual tonnage of stores was over 10,000, including forage for the horses. Not surprisingly, both the camp commissariat and South Eastern Railway were much in favour of a branch line to the camp and various proposals were put forward, but these were rejected by the War Office and the line was never built. Instead, the station at Sandgate became popular with the military; situated at the foot of Hospital Hill it was as near to the camp as Shorncliffe Station but was more convenient for invalid troops destined for the nearby Military Hospital.

Sandgate Station. Until it closed in 1929, the station was the principle embarkation point for troops from Shorncliffe camp.

Until it closed in 1929 Sandgate station was an icon of patriotism as soldiers departed for or arrived home from overseas duties. It was at this station that, at the end of November 1879, Captain Warren Wynne arrived to take command of the 2nd Field Company of Royal Engineers, stationed at Shorncliffe. Earlier that year, British forces in the Cape had been massacred by King Cetewayo's Zulus at Isandhlwana. This was followed by the famous defence of Rorke's Drift and the government had ordered more troops should be sent to the quell the uprising. When Captain Wynne arrived at Shorncliffe he found, *'Everything here is in the most awful state of confusion. The authorities have given orders and counter orders to such an extent that there is no knowing how to turn'*. After a few days of frantic preparations, Wynne's 125 strong company was ready to embark; the wagons at Sandgate station were loaded on the afternoon of the 30th November, with the men marching out of camp the following morning, marching down the hill to the accompaniment of the fifes and drums of the Guards and the band of the 45th Regiment. The train took them to Sheerness docks where the troops embarked upon the SS Walmer Castle, their destination being Cape Town and the Zulu Wars. Captain Wynne and his Royal Engineers saw action on several fronts eventually finding themselves under siege at Fort Eshowe. Although able to defend themselves from the Zulus, the men had less fortune fighting off illness. Several of the company succumbed before Wynne, who had now been promoted to Major, died on his 36th birthday, April 9th, 1879.

In 1882 the people of Sandgate turned out to welcome home the Royal Artillery from war in Egypt, an event reported in the Folkestone Herald,

> ARRIVAL OF TROOPS AT SANDGATE
> A large number of people went down to the station. Sandgate turned out quite gay with its flags. There were very good banners. Mr Simonds had two; one "See the conquering heroes come," and another "Welcome home to the hearty heroes of Tel-el-Kebir."

Unfortunately, the train which was due to arrive at 5.00 pm did not pull in until the early hours of the next morning, by which time all of the well-wishers had retired, so the event had to be re-enacted again a few days later.

Local well-wishers were busy again eight years later. The end of Queen Victoria's reign saw Britain embroiled in the second Boer War, a war which was to mark the turning point between the old set piece battles and cavalry charges of the past, and the warfare of artillery and trenches which would become the hallmark of the First World War. With misplaced confidence Britain expected that, with her numerically superior forces, it would not take long to defeat the Boer commandos. It was not to be that easy; the enemy, armed with the fine Mauser rifle, was a master of fieldcraft and avoided the feared British bayonet whenever possible. The British were to pay a high price before peace terms were agreed, and it was not long before the people of Sandgate were turning out to welcome home the wounded. A flavour of the task facing the British was given to the readers of the Folkestone Herald in January 1900 when a letter from Sergeant J. Munckton of the Royal East Kent Mounted Rifles was published,

Royal East Kent Mounted Rifles. The Folkestone Troop who went to fight in South Africa. Sergeant Munckton is seated on the far right of the middle row.

We have been in the battle of Colenso. It is terrible work to

see the men and horses drop dead around you. I was lucky enough to get out alright. The bullets simply hailed around us...Our officer was shot through the lungs. I had to shoot two horses that had been wounded. One bullet struck the ground about a foot in front of my horse as we were retreating. We are expecting another battle every day. We are waiting for reinforcements to come up. The water is running very short here. We shall have to force our way into Ladysmith or retire from here. Dysentery has broken out among the troops through bad water and the heat is intense. We are as black as Indians. I met a young fellow I know in the Royal Dragoons, lying next to us. They, too, are commencing to lose their horses from sickness. The English horses cannot stand the climate...I am afraid it is going to be a longer war than they think for. The country is so hilly and the Boers such good shots. I am keeping well up to now. Some of the troopers are gentlemen by birth. It is a rough life, and I shall be glad when it is over, if I get through alright.

Throughout 1900 trains full of wounded continued to arrive at Sandgate Station from where the seriously ill were taken to Shorncliffe Military Hospital, and those who had made some recovery were taken to the Beach Rocks convalescent home, situated on Sandgate seafront. Again, these arrivals were reported with patriotic enthusiasm in the local press,

Boer War soldiers at Sandgate. The arrival of wounded at Sandgate Station during 1900 always brought out welcoming crowds.

ARRIVAL OF MORE WOUNDED AT SANDGATE

On Sunday afternoon Sandgate Station was again the scene of excitement. All along the banks and on the platform were crowds of people, both civilian and military. About 3.30 the signal bell rang, and soon after the white smoke from the engine was to be seen between the hills towards Hythe. Inside was discerned parchment nut brown heroes lounging or sitting…the doors flew open and the inmates hobbled out and received a hearty cheer from the spectators. The invalids seemed to brighten and smiles were to be seen on their tan faces when the crowds of soldiers and civilians cheered them under the archway and along the parade, where the sea breeze blew against them and warm thick khaki coats had to be worn. At Beach Rocks they descended and went into the convalescent home where an entertainment and tea was provided.

One of the soldiers brought to Beach Rocks was 23 year-old Private Charlie Ward of the King's Own Yorkshire Light Infantry. He was suffering from severe wounds sustained on the 26th June 1900 at Lindley where his actions won him the Victoria Cross. He and his comrades were part of an outlying picquet surrounded and pinned down by 500 Boers. With two officers wounded, and all but six of the party dead or wounded, Charlie volunteered to take a message to a signalling station to call for help. His offer was initially refused because of the practical certainty that he would be shot in the attempt. As the situation

Private Charlie Ward VC. The 23 year-old was brought to the Beach Rocks in Sandgate to recover from his wounds.

became increasingly desperate, Charlie was given permission to go for help, and made the dash across 150 yards of open ground under a hail of fire. Having reached his destination unscathed and delivered his message, he left the safety of the station and ran back to let the men know that the message had been delivered and that help was on the way. It was on the return trip that Charlie's luck ran out and he was hit several times. After his recovery at Sandgate, Private Ward received his medal from Queen Victoria, with the added distinction that he was the last person ever to receive the award from her hands.

The people of Folkestone were, as always, quick to rally to the support of the invalid soldiers; for those fit enough a summer concert was arranged at the Victoria Pier where a collection produced £2.10s for the purchase of tobacco and cigarettes for the men. Curiously, whilst the troops were in hospital or convalescing, they were unable to draw their pay to

Boer War Concert at Shorncliffe. Held in the camp gymnasium on the 23rd November 1899 to raise funds for the wives and children of soldiers and sailors fighting in South Africa. The programme carries the motto 'One Flag, and One Throne'.

buy their own cigarettes. The Folkestone Herald on the 14th July 1900 put out an emotional appeal for support,

> Visitors who are enjoying the beautiful air of Folkestone, I ask you not to forget the tobacco pipe of these poor weak and jaded soldiers down in Sandgate. We made a huge fuss of 'Tommy Atkins' when he departed for the front in good health; let us try to remember him now that he is down in health and spirits. It has fairly made my heart bleed lately to hear the tale of suffering of some of these men.

Scout of the Royal Dragoons. Seen here proudly wearing his two Boer War campaign medals

The men who returned unharmed from the Boer Wars were the first to enjoy the benefits of the new barrack buildings at Shorncliffe camp. The Royal Dragoons had spent three years in South Africa and when they returned to Shorncliffe in 1902 they had an extra recruit; his name was Scout. He had enlisted almost as soon as the Dragoons had landed at Durban harbour in November 1899. The men had disembarked and were preparing to eat their rations when they were joined by a puppy scrounging for food. Soldiers have always had a soft spot for animals and they were happy to share their food with the visitor. Returning to the same spot the next morning the dog discovered that the troops had already boarded the train for their journey inland but, at the last minute, a carriage door opened and in he hopped. The dog joined the Dragoons in their camp at Pietermaritzburg and when the regiment rode out he took up position at the front of the column thus earning the name Scout. It was at the battle of Spion Kop that Scout saw his first action, twice crossing the Tugela River with the troops; once on dry land he would take up his position at the head of the cavalry, no doubt to the surprise of the Boers.

When peace was declared Scout marched proudly at the front of his regiment as they entered Bloemfontein and he led them into Cape Town where they were to embark for the voyage home. Needless to say, not a single dragoon would contemplate leaving Scout behind and he returned to England where, after quarantine, he rejoined his regiment at Shorncliffe. For his services during the war Scout was awarded the Queen's South Africa Medal with six bars and the King's South Africa Medal with two bars.

It is not recorded whether Scout was on parade in late 1902, but the Royal Dragoons were; over a thousand mounted troops were inspected at Shorncliffe by the German Kaiser. Mounted on his white charger, Queen Victoria's grandson was accompanied by Field Marshall Lord Roberts, the acclaimed leader of the British in the Boer Wars. Little did anyone then anticipate that the gleaming military helmet worn by the Kaiser would soon come to symbolise the dreaded 'Hun'.

The Kaiser visits Shorncliffe 1902. In lashing rain the Kaiser, astride the white horse, inspected the Shorncliffe men, including the Royal Dragoons.

With the passing of the Victorian era, the British army was beginning to recognise the need to provide modern facilities and opportunities for its soldiers; their welfare was provided for with the creation of soldiers' institutes and temperance organisations were encouraged to convey to the men the benefits of abstinence. Even so, there was the occasional lament for the past, as recorded by this old soldier on a visit to Shorncliffe in 1898:

> I ascended the hill and gained Shorncliffe Camp, which appeared to be deadly dull. On the western side the old wooden huts are demolished, and on the north the old and empty buildings are all painted with a great white cross which spells 'condemned'. Soon the old wooden huts which have stood the winter gales of nearly fifty years will have disappeared from view.
>
> I could not help thinking as I gazed on these melancholy looking dwellings of the thousands of brave fellows who have tenanted the huts from time to time. Scores, many hundred of them must have laid down their lives for us – some have died in foreign lands from disease, some have been shot down in battle with their faces turned on the foe, under scorching sun or in

End of an Era. A photo of the last of the huts at Shorncliffe erected during the Crimean War, just before it was demolished to make way for new brick barracks in 1899.

mountain passes covered with eternal snow.

Before my mind there passes, as I write, a procession of the brave men who have lived here – I think of them as they were – I think of the happy hours I have spent in their company. Where are they now? Gone, alas, for ever.

The Volunteer Movement

Before we progress to the twentieth century, there is one more phenomenon to consider; the Volunteer Movement. The Napoleonic Wars had seen a patriotic rush to arms, although some who had joined the volunteers of that time had done so in the hope of avoiding service in the regular army. The regular British Army which, as we have seen, was drastically cut after 1815, spent most of its time policing the far flung parts of the British Empire. The toll exacted by the Crimean War and, to a lesser extent, the Indian Mutiny in 1857, meant that when the country was unexpectedly threatened again in 1859, there was controlled panic at the prospect of having to defend our shores. It was Napoleon III, Bonaparte's nephew, who was now Emperor of France and trouble was brewing on the continent between France and Austria. Britain had no reason to be concerned; after all she had fought alongside the French in the Crimea. In the hope of succeeding where his much more talented uncle had failed, and using as an excuse Britain's criticism of French Republicanism, Napoleon started to move troops to the Channel coast in preparation for a planned invasion. In a replay of events of 50 years earlier, the British were roused into action and men flocked to form and join volunteer units. Locally, the call to arms was led by the Mayors of Folkestone and Hythe, and between the towns there was some friendly

Folkestone Volunteer Rifle Corps.

Sir,

The Committee appointed at a Public Meeting, held on the 19th May, to ascertain the cost of an Equipment for each Volunteer, having obtained the required information, it is proposed to hold a Public Meeting, on Tuesday, the 21st Inst., in the Sessions Hall, at 7 o'Clock, p.m., for the purpose of communicating the particulars.

In order to give effect to the unanimous wish of the Meeting, held on 19th May, for the formation of a Rifle Corps, it will be necessary at this Meeting to arrange for the enlistment of Volunteers, and such other matters as may be deemed expedient.

Your co-operation and attendance is earnestly solicited, as the establishment of Volunteer Rifle and Artillery Corps, is unquestionably of the highest importance in a Local as well as a National point of view.

I have the honor to be,

Sir,

Your obedient Servant,

GILBERT KENNICOTT,

Mayor.

Folkestone,
13th June, 1859.

Call to Arms. A letter from Folkestone's mayor calling a meeting at the Sessions Hall on the 21st June 1859, to enlist Volunteers into the Folkestone Volunteer Rifle Corps.

rivalry as to who could muster the largest force. At a rally in May 1859, at Folkestone's Sessions House, a Mr. Browell addressed the gathering with feeling,

I am not an alarmist but this is a subject that demands attention from us all as loyal subjects of the Queen. I can assure you that it is far from my wish to convey an impression that we have cause to fear a foreign invasion, or to say anything likely to create a panic; still it is impossible for us to observe what is passing on the continent of Europe without feeling a probability that we shall be drawn into it — a crisis has arisen and it becomes every man to use his best endeavours to protect our country from a foreign invasion.

Not surprisingly, the response to this masterly speech, so full of Victorian innuendo, was immediate and the Folkestone Rifle Volunteers were formed. At a subsequent meeting in the King's Arms Assembly Rooms (later to be the site of the Queens Hotel, and now Queens House) in Guildhall Street, Captain A.M.Leith, was elected commander of the Corps and the other officers and NCOs chosen. Arrangements were put in hand for clothing, equipping and training the men, and appeals for public financial support were issued. In September 1859 the Rifle Volunteers were joined by volunteer artillery (styled the 3rd Kent Artillery Volunteers), a band of men formed with the support of the Lord Lieutenant of Kent, who thought that the country had enough rifle corps and that the artillerymen, who could man the rearmed Martello Towers and Bayle

Captain A.M.Leith. In command of the Folkestone Rifle Volunteers, he was also manager of the town's National Provincial Bank.

Fort, would be much more effective in repelling an invasion. The result was that, once again, the coast bristled with rifles and cannon and, at weekends, the men would take up their arms and re-enact the rehearsals of their grandfathers. However, Napoleon III, like his uncle, never launched his invasion; a few years later, after losing a war with the Prussians, he fell from grace and fled to England to live out the rest of his life in exile. For one whose family name had for half a century been the bane of the protectors of the Kentish coast, it is ironic that Napoleon III spent his last years at Chislehurst in Kent, until his death in 1873.

Queen's Hotel, Folkestone. Situated at the junction of Guildhall Street and Sandgate Road, this is where Captain Gosling and his men had their farewell dinner before leaving for the Boer War.

As for the volunteers, they continued to thrive, despite opposition from the regular military authorities, and eventually they were put on a regular footing. The Folkestone and Hythe Rifle Volunteers were incorporated into the 2nd Cinque Ports Battalion which, in 1874, was consolidated into the 5th East Kent Rifle Volunteers and which, in its turn, became the 1st Volunteer Battalion, East Kent Regiment (The Buffs). In January 1900, the Buffs, under Captain Arthur Gosling (whose father had been one of the founders of the Rifle Volunteers in 1859), volunteered for service in the Boer War and, together with the Folkestone contingent of the Royal East Kent Mounted Rifles, they were treated to a patriotic send off. First there was a farewell dinner at the Queens Hotel in Guildhall Street,

Artillery Volunteers 1860. Seen practising with a cannon atop a Martello Tower at Hythe.

with speeches, toasts and entertainment. A few days later, Captain Gosling marched his men from their barracks at the School of Musketry in Hythe, past cheering crowds of children who had been given the day off school, through Sandgate and into Coolinge Lane to entrain at Shorncliffe Station, where they were given a final bon voyage. A commemorative plaque to Captain Gosling and his men can be seen on the tower of Christ Church in Folkestone, being all that remains of the church following a direct hit during the Second World War.

The Artillery Volunteers also continued well after the threat of this latest Napoleonic invasion had passed. Along the south coast, the various batteries were formed into corps, with Folkestone becoming 2nd Corps in 1870. Hythe, however, was unable to maintain an effective strength and was disbanded in 1860. Training took place on cannons mounted on Martello Towers and at the Bayle Battery in Folkestone.

As well as the volunteer artillery and infantry units, there was a third element; the mounted volunteers. With a pedigree stretching back to 1794, and various changes in name, the East Kent Mounted Rifles were already well established during the Victorian period. At a spectacular review held at Mote Park in 1837, in honour of Queen Victoria's accession, D Troop based at Hythe formed part of the Brigade of over 600 men of the East and West Kent Mounted Yeomanry. On the occasion of the royal visit to Shorncliffe in August 1855 (see Chapter 5), the East Kent Regiment of Yeomanry Cavalry formed the Guard of Honour for the Queen and Consort on their ride from Folkestone to the camp and back. The following year saw the Regiment being awarded the privilege of adding 'Royal' to its title. The appointment of the Duke of Connaught as Honorary Colonel in 1873 led to his name also being added to the Regiment's title. At Queen Victoria's centenary celebrations in 1897, the Regiment was represented by a detachment of nine other ranks under the command of Major E. Frewen; they proudly joined other yeomanry cavalry in lining the Mall.

During the Boer War period and up to the start of the Great War, the Regiment held its annual training at Shorncliffe camp. Organised now into four squadrons totalling over 300 men, the Folkestone Troop, alongside those from Ashford and the Weald, formed D Squadron. As we have seen, the East Kent Mounted Rifles served with the Imperial Yeomanry in the Boer War.

In 1908, the various elements of the Volunteer Movement[15] were incorporated into the Territorial Force, and aligned with their regular county regiments, although they proudly clung onto their existing regimental titles where they could. With the outbreak of war in 1914, the Territorials were formed into battalions where they fought alongside their comrades in the Regular Army.

[15] For an interesting account of the history of the Volunteer Movement, see Appendix H.

Friday the 20th May 1837, a review at Mote Park in Maidstone to celebrate Victoria's accession to the throne. This fine engraving shows 600 volunteers of the East and West Kent Regiments of Yeomanry Cavalry, including D Troop from Hythe.

Chapter 8

THE GREAT WAR

With the death of Queen Victoria in 1901, the twentieth century dawned. The relief at the ending of the Boer War was palpable and as a sense of peace returned to the country the south coast continued to attract the gentility and, increasingly, the emerging middle classes. New hotels and guest houses were springing up to cater for the visitors, for whom promenading along the Leas in Folkestone, or the Royal Military Canal and gardens in Hythe, were almost compulsory. The marching bands from Shorncliffe Garrison, and the smaller military ensembles to be seen performing in the Hythe and Folkestone bandstands, were colourful and ever popular. Shorncliffe Camp which, until 1914, still allowed fairly free access to the public,

March Past. A regular pre-war sight. These soldiers are marching along Sandgate Road, Folkestone, towards what is now the top of the pedestrian precinct.

provided a constant source of entertainment and grandeur, with its parades by the cavalry, artillery and infantry. The pre-war Ward Lock guide placed the camp very much on the itinerary, recommending that, *'The cavalry stables, the artillery gun sheds, the riding school and the gymnasium can all be seen by visitors to the Camp. If the visit is made in the morning, there will probably be an opportunity of witnessing drills or evolutions of some kind on the extensive camp ground.'* The area continued to prosper.

The accession of King George V and Queen Mary in 1911 was cause for nationwide celebrations; peace and prosperity seemed unending. Every year Folkestone became the willing host of regular and volunteer army units on their annual training exercises and, at Hythe, the School of Musketry brought its

11th Hussars in 1909. The men of the 11th Hussars, and their dog, snapped at Shorncliffe in 1909. In 1856 members of the same regiment had been at the camp after their return from the Crimea where they had taken part in the Charge of the Light Brigade.

own military visitors. With the arrival of the cinema, the opportunities for entertainment were unsurpassed. The trend was set by the Pleasure Gardens Theatre which hosted the very first open air cinema showing in the country. In 1910, the Electric (later the Savoy) opened next door to the Town Hall followed, in 1912, by no less than three more cinemas; the Queen's in Tontine Street, the Playhouse in Guildhall Street and the Central Picture Theatre in George Lane. Cheriton had acquired its own cinema in 1911, the Electric Hall on the High Street. Even Hythe, which had something of a reputation for resistance to change from its army of retired colonels, succumbed and provided a cinema at the eastern end of its High Street. Sandgate, however, remained loyal to live entertainment provided by the Alhambra Theatre of Varieties[16]. Armed with the Ward Lock guide, the visitor could plan his week; in Hythe a day's bowls would cost 6d, whilst 18 holes of golf at the course to the west of the town would cost 2/6d. Season tickets for cricket and croquet cost 21s and 15s respectively. The choice of activities in Folkestone seemed limitless. There were Turkish baths, public baths and private baths as well, of course,

Pre-war Folkestone. This busy seaside scene was typical of Edwardian Folkestone. The Victoria Pier is in the background.

as sea bathing for which the Noah's Ark bathing machines could be hired. For the family, there was the recommendation that, *'Juvenile paddlers seem to prefer that part of the beach which is in front of the switchback railway.'* However, unnoticed by the country at large, stormclouds were gathering across Europe. In truth, the warning signs had been there since the end of the Franco-Prussian wars, but few realised just how fragile the age of peace really was.

Before the outbreak of the Great War Shorncliffe camp was a popular and modern establishment. The new barracks were comfortable and camp amenities unrivalled; add in the south coast climate and sea air and it is little wonder that a posting to Folkestone was eagerly sought. The 1st Battalion, Royal Warwickshire Regiment had been lucky, they had been at Shorncliffe since 1912. In command of the 10th Brigade, which included the Royal Warwicks, the Royal Irish Fusiliers and the Seaforth Highlanders was Brigadier Aylmer Haldane. His diary of the two years leading up to the outbreak of war contains a number of amusing entries,

1913

19th February

Capt. Mansfield who is in arrest for money troubles, last
night broke his arrest and went out and slew a cock and six
hens belonging to Colonel Churcher. He is now in close

---

[16] The Alhambra underwent several changes of name; in 1867 it became the Alexandra Hotel and Music Hall, followed by Maltby's Mansion of Mirth, finally Hill's Hall of Hilarity in 1897.

arrest, and I think will have to be placed under observation for madness.

5th March

Capt. Mansfield not having paid his mess bill will now be ordered to resign.

31st March

Spoke to Col. Campbell regarding bad behaviour of his regiment at Hythe. If it continues I shall either have larger picquets or put it out of bounds. Capt. Mansfield 1/Royal Irish Fusiliers has been removed from the Army. He was a useless and bad officer. Capt. Stewart-Robinson – 2/Seaforth Highlanders, a weak and dissolute person, has sent in his papers and will be a good riddance.

Haldane's contempt for poor leadership was not confined to junior officers. His comments about his senior officer, Major-General Thomas D'Oyly Snow, reveal a man who was indiscriminate in his criticism.

3rd May

The G.O.C. 4th Division (Snow) again showed his ignorance of any tactical principles and had we not been fighting an imaginary enemy (territorial troops) we should certainly have been beaten; as it was the fight was considered drawn whereas by massing against the enemy's nearest flank he could have been routed. General Snow ignored the principles of economy of force, of direction (of) the mass and security. He, however, was quite pleased with himself.

The hard-pressed Brigadier had to contend not only with drunken troops and incompetent officers; his high standards were also tested by the presence of a mascot at that year's Trooping of the Colour at Shorncliffe Camp.

24th May

Warwicks very slow. I dislike their black buck

The Royal Warwickshire Regiment. Here seen parading at Shorncliffe with their mascot, an antelope. Brigadier Haldane was unimpressed by the need to pull the antelope along at the Trooping of the Colour.

which they have on ceremonial parades. Today, it had to be dragged past. Too much circus about it.

During the summer of 1913, more training exercises were held, but with limited success,

24th July
Then on to see the Royal Irish Fusiliers who were very leisurely about doing their work. Churcher had not reconnoitred the ground in advance and the attack was spoilt by a hay-field. He blamed the hay-field for being there not himself. I corrected him. There is too much 'eye-wash' about this battalion...

26th August
Had 2/Royal Dublin Fusiliers in main attack. Some officers are very stupid at grasping an order, no matter how clearly and carefully given.

There were a few officers who satisfied Haldane's high standards but, when it came, the brigadier's praise was sparing,

4th September
Col. Bradford and Maj. Elkington lead their battalions well. Mainwaring commanded in defence satisfactorily.

By June of 1914, Haldane's diary was reflecting a general improvement in the condition and qualities of the men under his command. The three regiments at

Shorncliffe, together with the 3rd (King's Own) Hussars would soon be glad of the exacting demands imposed by their commander. In an interesting footnote to history, it was Brigadier-General Haldane who led the call for a memorial at Shorncliffe to Sir John Moore. By the summer of 1914 the architect, Sir Aston Webb had designed the hall which could hold 300 men and

The 3rd Hussars parade through Folkestone. This photo was taken on the 20th June when the 3rd Hussars were parading through the town before local dignitaries. Within 2 months these troops embarked for France as part of the British Expeditionary Force. Few of them returned.

the sculptor, John Tweed, had been commissioned to create the bronze statue of the great general. The Folkestone Herald of the 6th June 1914 carried a sketch of the memorial, with the announcement that a further £900 was needed to fund the construction, and inviting donations. The outbreak of war two months later was to delay the building of the memorial for several years but, even when he was commanding the 3rd Division in the Ypres salient during 1915, Aylmer Haldane did not forget his project; he rescued from the ruins of the village church at Zillebeke the fallen weather cock, sent it home and it was placed on the roof of the Sir John Moore Memorial Library, which was eventually opened on the 5th July 1923, and where it can still be seen. Writing in 1922, Lieutenant General Haldane recalled his time at Shorncliffe,

> It fell to me to command the 10th Infantry Brigade at Shorncliffe for the two and a half years prior to the war, and on the historic ground where Moore trained the famous Light Brigade – troops whose excellence has never been surpassed, if indeed equalled in any Army – it would have been difficult not to have felt inspired to try to make the British soldier of today a worthy successor of his ancestor of Peninsular times.

The people of Folkestone had become used to the sound of the northern burr and Irish brogue and in the evenings the haunting sound of bagpipes drifted across the town. Just before the August Bank Holiday weekend of 1914 large crowds, families and friends, as well as local people, gathered at Shorncliffe for the annual inter-regimental sports day. Little did anyone know that, following a single gunshot in Sarajevo, within a few days the young men now doing battle on the sports field would be heading for France, and a battle from which few of them would return.

One of the officers responsible for organising the sports day was the Adjutant of the Royal Warwicks. It was a role he had first undertaken with the regiment in India. Whilst at Shorncliffe he had also passed the Officers' Course at the Hythe School of Musketry. When his Battalion left the camp for the Western Front in August, he accompanied them, and took part in a number of actions over the following weeks. Taking up an advance position before his company entered a small village, this young officer took a sniper's bullet; it entered his back, piercing his lung and exited the front. His men could not reach him until dark due to sniper fire. Promoted to Captain in the field, he was also awarded the DSO for 'Conspicuous gallantry leading on 13 October, when he turned the enemy out of the trenches with the bayonet. He was severely wounded.' The officer's name was Bernard Law Montgomery and, having survived the war, he returned to Shorncliffe with his old battalion in 1925. A senior officer recalled "... Monty coming to the battalion in 1925 and spending about a year with us at Shorncliffe. Even in those days every body recognised the fact that he would go to the top of his profession – a rare bird in that he *was a chap who was not only very astute of himself – but he'd really studied the business of soldiering, which not many people did in those days – not in the dedicated sense."* Montgomery became a household name during the Second World War after his victory over Rommel at El Alamein.

The inter-regimental sports day did not include cricket, which was a shame for the Seaforth Highlanders; their Colonel was Evelyn Bradford (the same officer mentioned earlier with approval in the diaries of Aylmer Haldane). In peacetime, he was a county cricketer, playing for Hampshire as opening bat and with a reputation as a fast bowler. Against the Australians at Southampton in 1899 he hit 102 with the next highest scorer managing only 39. He had joined the army before the war and continued with his cricket, invariably putting in a high scoring innings. In the match between Shorncliffe Garrison and Folkestone in May 1913 he hit 251. Colonel Bradley left Shorncliffe with his battalion in August 1914 for the Western Front. He was killed in action at Soissons on the 14th September 1914 at the age of 45.

Belgian Refugees 1914. A rare picture of some of the Belgians who managed to escape to Folkestone from the German invasion of their country. Many thousands were welcomed to the town and provided with homes.

In two contrasting events, the people of Folkestone were the first in Britain to witness realities of the war; on the 4th August 1914, a few days even before war was declared, fishing boats and coal carriers started to arrive in the harbour carrying the first pitiful cargoes of human refugees. They had escaped from Belgium as their country was overrun and were the first of many thousands soon to flood the town. *"There were mothers who had been hounded from home and country before they could gather the little ones in their arms"*, and who had no idea where their children might be and, *"Girls with flushed cheeks and wild terrified eyes whose stories others whispered under their breath. They were the victims of German lust."* Folkestone took these people to its heart and found homes and security for many thousands of Belgians during the war. On the 7th September, the first issue of Le Franco-Belge de Folkestone was published. Printed in French this newspaper gave the refugees information about the war, advertised lodgings and other services and, most important, listed names of all arrivals from Belgium in the hope that families and friends would be able to trace each other. It was not just the civilian refugees who arrived in the town; on the 13th October two thousand Belgian troops arrived from Ostend. Many had come straight from the fight to defend their country and their wounds were often roughly dressed. Hotels were immediately commandeered, with visitors being given immediate notice, and all local motor cars were called upon to collect the wounded from the harbour and take them to the hastily vacated hotels for treatment. The other event watched by the people of Folkestone, but with less sympathy, was the rounding up of several hundred German and Austrian men. They were reservists with the armies of those countries and upon the declaration of war had arrived at Folkestone harbour in the hope of finding a ship out of England. Troops and police were despatched to round up these men who were marched through the town and into captivity for the duration.

By the end of September there were nearly 20,000 recruits in training at Shorncliffe. The place had lost its peacetime calm and visitors would now watch the hustle of preparations for war instead of taking a leisurely stroll across St Martin's Plain. The regular soldiers had left with the British Expeditionary Force and the men now at Shorncliffe were the bank clerks, students, farm labourers and street hawkers who would form the backbone of Kitchener's Army. All over the country young men were rushing to join up spurred on by talk that the war might 'be over by Christmas'. The Folkestone MP, Sir Phillip Sassoon, led the appeal locally with great success, especially from among the East Kent Yeomanry, with which he was serving. The recruits from around the country were arriving at Shorncliffe in their thousands. Every day on the Leas men could be seen taking gunnery instruction, even before receiving their guns or uniforms, whilst at Shorncliffe camp they learned drill and bayonet practice. At Seabrook, just below Shorncliffe, trenches were dug for the men to practice 'going over the top'.

The new barracks at Shorncliffe could not accommodate all of the men; huts and tents began to spring up on St. Martin's Plain and at Dibgate. The Folkestone Herald of the 16th October 1914 reported that wooden huts had been hastily erected in the grounds of the country mansion at Sandling by 350 workmen to house 8000 men of Kitchener's Army. It was perhaps an unintended foretaste of conditions in the trenches that the camp was knee

Sandling Station and Camp. Built initially for Kitchener's Men, Sandling camp became home for tens of thousands of Canadians. In this picture, the only activity is a few sheep on the hills and the steam tractor in the foreground.

deep in mud. During the early days of the War, men from the Yorkshire and Lancashire Regiment and the Queen's Regiment were quartered at East and West Sandling camps. Even these camps could not accommodate all of the men and many were billeted in local hotels and homes. The home comforts provided by the landladies of Folkestone must have been welcome to the men after a hard day of training and for many of whom this was the first time away from home. After basic training in Aldershot, the men of the 8th Battalion of the Leicestershire Regiment arrived in Folkestone early in 1915 and were billeted in houses on the Leas and along Sandgate Road, whilst their pals in the 9th Battalion were quartered along the coast at New Romney. The Leicester 'Tigers' were a typical example of the new army of lads eager to respond to the call to arms. Dick Read had been an engineering apprentice in Leicester before finding himself one day standing in the queue of the recruiting office with a number of other hopefuls. Read was with the 8th Battalion and remembered his time in Folkestone before departing for the Front; especially he recalled *"...long route marches in full equipment. Our Battalion became a reality, and I'm sure the survivors of the 110th Brigade will never forget the long and arduous ascents of the hill on the Dover Road, with the 'Valiant Sailor' at the summit, and the Capel turn."*

Home from Home. These men of Kitchener's Army found billets in Folkestone homes.

Soldiers were also billeted in Hythe and along the coast in towns and villages of the Romney Marsh. Lydd already had an established army presence; during the 1880s land had been acquired by the Board of Ordnance for artillery training and testing. The local residents had long been accustomed to the deafening noise of the big guns firing on the ranges, and perhaps the young men of Kitchener's Army billeted with the Marsh folk drew some benefit from the experience before they found themselves in the nightmare of the Western Front.

The insatiable hunger of the Western Front for these young men ensured that, no sooner had one shipload of troops left Folkestone harbour for France, than the next detachment were made ready. For those Folkestone families who billeted the men it must have been distressing to wave off one after the other knowing that many of them would never return home. As the war progressed, more and more troops arrived in Folkestone. For many the stay was all too brief, little more than a day or two before embarkation.

Lydd Camp 1916. The town has military connections going back centuries, but Lydd Camp came into being in the 1880s. A new explosive was developed there and christened Lyddite.

To cater for the soldiers in transit rest camps were built. They were ugly blocks of houses enclosed by corrugated iron and soon their stark profiles dominated the west end of the town; the first was erected in January 1916 in Marine Terrace and slept 2200 men; Rest Camp No 2 went up five months later off Bathurst Road equipped with tents heated by a stove and a large YMCA hut. The largest camp was No 3 which opened in early 1917 and took in a large area of the Leas including Clifton Crescent and Earls Avenue and which catered for 5000 men. At their peak, the camps were seeing in excess of 10,000 men passing through every day. Despite their lack of architectural charm, the rest camps were a haven for the men for many of whom it was to be their last sleeping place on English soil. As they set off for war each man was given either a copy of the New Testament or the Book of Psalms.

It was not only the soldiers who were training; the Metropole Hotel on Folkestone's Leas became the headquarters for the WAACs. Seven thousand of these volunteer female auxiliaries were trained as cooks, waitresses, clerks, mechanics and motorists before receiving their inoculations and setting off for duties overseas.

Number 3 Rest Camp, the Leas. One of five such camps, this was one of the largest. Surrounded by corrugated iron, it was not attractive to look at but provided a welcome respite for many thousands of men on their way to the Western Front.

If the people of Folkestone had begun to adjust to hearing accents from every corner of the British Isles, they were soon to hear altogether a new sound; the Canadians were coming. Within two days of war being declared the Canadian government offered to send troops and the First Contingent of 33,000 men set sail in October 1914. They were quartered on Salisbury Plain where they found themselves enjoying the delights of an English winter; incessant rain and mud over their boots. Meanwhile, in Canada,

Shop, Number 3 Rest Camp. A fascinating picture of the shop provided for the soldiers. Among the items for sale were regimental sweetheart badges, trench powder, pynka and French phrase books. The owl on the shelf is for a display of Ingersoll watches.

the Second Contingent was being formed and when they arrived in the spring and summer of 1915 they were brought to Shorncliffe. By the end of the year there were 40,000 Canadians living and training in Folkestone and Hythe; it was said that the area had become a suburb of Toronto.

Private Vince Colley, CEF. Having emigrated to Canada, he returned to England with the Canadian Army in 1915. Vince, seated, was killed in action shortly after going to the front

These men were all volunteers; they did not have to fight to protect their own country thousands of miles away. The courage and tenacity of the Canadians at Vimy Ridge and Neuve Chapelle are indelibly remembered with the endless rows of headstones in the cemeteries in northern France and Belgium each one bearing the proud emblem of the maple leaf. Many of these brave young men no doubt answered the call to arms out of a sense of loyalty to the mother country. Private Vince Colley may have been typical. He was born at Wickhamford near Evesham in Worcestershire on the 18th January 1894 and emigrated to Canada in 1911, where he worked on the Canadian Pacific

Railway. Private Colley joined the 32nd Infantry Battalion, Manitoba & Saskatchewan, part of the Second Contingent, and came to Shorncliffe for his training. Whilst here he sent a postcard home to his family in Wickhamford with a picture of 'Tin Town' (Risborough Barracks) on the front, and saying that he hoped to visit his family shortly. It is hoped that he did; Private Colley was killed in action on the 12th June 1916.

The men had some basic training at camps in Canada, but the real work was done whilst in England. Additional practice trenches were dug near Sandling Station; there was grenade throwing and bayonet practice and, of course, marching. Opinion seems to have been divided on the value of these exercises. Private Donald Fraser wrote in his Journal: *"Friday September 17 1915: After four months training in Kent, England, where we had a very enjoyable time, first at Dibgate in the vicinity of Shorncliffe, then at Lydd where we had a rush shooting practice . . . we were considered fit and skilled in the art of warfare, ready to meet the hated Hun. When I think of it, our training was decidedly amateurish and impractical. It consisted mainly of route marches and alignment movements. Our musketry course amounted to nothing; we had only half an idea about the handling of bombs. We were perfectly ignorant regarding rifle grenades."* In contrast, Captain J.W. Margeson of the 25th Nova Scotia Infantry Battalion wrote home to his local newspaper on the 9th September 1915, *"East Sandling. Our camp is beautifully situated, sheltered between the hills in the County of Kent. In this valley about 75,000 Canadian boys are in training. All the men have had their practice at the Hythe shooting ranges, which are looked upon as the finest in the world. Trench warfare has been undertaken and it would surprise you to see how quickly the 25th Battalion can 'dig themselves in' and prepare to meet the foe. Much more has been accomplished which I am not privileged at this time to make known. However, you can take it from me that the boys are ready — prepared to fight, prepared to die if necessary for the preservation of those liberties which Canadians have enjoyed across the seas."*

On the 2nd September 1915, the King, accompanied by Lord Kitchener, the Secretary of State for War, came to inspect the Canadians of the Second Contingent who paraded at Beachborough Park. Private Arthur Frier was among the troops reviewed. A farmer from New Brunswick, Frier had a liking for Donald McGill comic postcards, and sent one to his mother after the royal inspection, *"Dear Mother,*

Waiting for the King. September 1915. These men of the Canadian Expeditionary Force are taking a breather before the Royal entourage arrives at Beachborough to inspect the men prior to their departure for the front.

We were reviewed by the King and Kitchener today. It was quite a sight to see so many soldiers gathered together. We are having rather chilly wet weather these last few days. — Arthur." On the same day the farm lad also sent a separate postcard to his father, *"Dear Father, I received your letter and was glad to hear from you. I am glad to hear the crops are good and that you are getting them harvested without much extra work. They are cutting their grain here now. The greater part of it is gathered in. —*

Arthur." During his inspection of the Canadians the King had a message for the men,

> The past weeks at Shorncliffe have been for you a period of severe and rigorous training…History will never forget the loyalty and readiness with which you rallied to the aid of your Mother Country in the hour of danger. My thoughts will be with you. May God bless you and bring you victory.

After the inspection the King and his entourage rode through the streets of Cheriton to the cheers of the crowds.

The men trained hard and played hard. The camps tried to provide as much on-site recreation as possible. A tent for concert parties was set up at Caesar's Camp and opportunities for further education allowed a number of medical students, engineers and others to

The King riding through Cheriton. Having inspected the Canadians at Beachborough Park, the King rides through Cheriton to Shorncliffe Station. Lord Kitchener is riding the white horse alongside the King as they pass the White Lion and All Soul's School.

continue with their studies. With camps such as Dibgate, Sandling and Otterpool (near Lympne) being some distance from Folkestone and Hythe, it was a boon when, in early 1915, the Bank of England staff raised enough money to provide a YMCA hut at St. Martin's Plain. On weekdays concerts and films were provided and on Sundays religious services were held. There was a counter where the men could buy cigarettes and refreshments; writing paper and envelopes were provided free of charge. A gramophone and bagatelle table were also available. At Sandling, Mrs Fuller of Stone Farm and some friends opened the Jellicoe Club in two cottages opposite the camp entrance. The men could buy basic provisions and enjoy a cup of

Cheriton Electric Cinema. Very popular with the troops during the Great War, the Cinema doubled as the Palace Theatre, offering live entertainment in the form of vaudeville and wrestling, with two shows each night.

tea and a chat. After the war an oak cross was erected as a memorial to the Club and the men who used it. This was later replaced by a stone cross, built upon the original inscribed plinth, which can still be seen outside the present day Stone Farm. But there was also plenty off camp to attract the men. In Sandgate, the Alhambra Music Hall had closed in June 1914, but was taken over by the Canadian Red Triangle and used as a YMCA. In Cheriton, the

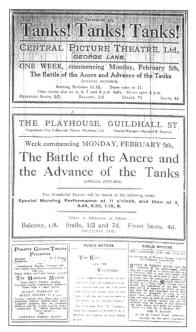

The 'Flicks' 1917. Without televisions, the public depended upon the cinema for film coverage of the war. Lighter fare was available at the Pleasure Gardens Theatre with the musical, The Marriage Market. Music was provided by the massed bands of the Canadian Army.

Electric Hall Cinema, which had opened in 1911, was ever popular with the troops, especially as the twice nightly bill at the 400-seater was supplemented by vaudeville, boxing and wrestling. A trip into Folkestone could be rewarded with a choice of cinemas or live entertainment at the Pleasure Gardens. Private G. Broome of the 32nd Battalion found time to learn a new skill. From Risborough Barracks he wrote to his mother in Canada: *"29th September 1915: We have had nice weather here till today and it's raining cats and dogs. We are fixed up alright though. We are in huts. About 30 men live in each hut and have their beds and tables and chairs and crockery. The food is brought from the cookhouse and we eat right in our huts. They are pretty big although the name makes one think they are small. I believe I told you we are near Folkestone. We go there nearly every night. I am learning to roller skate. It is great fun although kind of rough for a learner."* Private Broome left for France in early 1916. He was wounded but returned to active service when, on the 9th April 1917, he was wounded again at Vimy Ridge. He was shipped back to a military hospital in England but six months later, at the age of 20, George Broome died of his wounds.

In something of a break with the traditions of soldiers of previous generations, the behaviour of the Canadians and, for that matter, of all other troops, was exemplary. The incidents of drunkenness, so often the scourge of garrison towns, was very low; the Commanding Officer of the Canadians at Shorncliffe, Major-General Sir Sam Steele, was sufficiently impressed by his men's general behaviour that he withdrew the military police from Folkestone and put the men on their honour. However, one Folkestone resident, who was only seven years old at the time, remembers things differently; amidst a number of instances of drunkenness, F.W. Walker recalled a riot in Rendezvous Street when the MPs had to turn fire hoses on the men. There are very few instances of Canadian troops being brought before the town's justices; most seem to have involved breaching blackout regulations. Perhaps the most curious instance of misconduct involved Private William Head, who came up for judgement at the Maidstone Assizes in February 1916, on a charge of bigamy. The soldier made a strong appeal to the judge to be allowed to go to the front with his comrades. The judge seems to have been moved by this plea, and simply bound over Private Head to come up for judgment.

Then there is the rather delicate subject of female company. As well as providing a distraction for the newly arrived troops from the corners of England

and the Empire, the prospect of seeing the local girls was also comfort for the boys at the front, especially if they were lucky enough to catch a 'Blighty'. This was what happened to Private Jack Branch of the 28th (Northwest) Battalion. He was a member of a wiring party in No Man's Land when he took a shrapnel bullet through his arm. Although in great pain, he soon realised that the injury was not going to permanently disable him, but was bad enough to warrant his medical evacuation to England and, as he was carried out of the line by the stretcher-bearers, he cheerfully called to the rest of his platoon, *"I'll give your love to all the girls at Shorncliffe."* It was not just the local girls who could catch a soldier's eye; there were still many Belgian families in Folkestone. Private Charlie Thicke was stationed at Risborough Barracks waiting to be sent to the front in July 1915 when he wrote to his parents in Canada, *"Dear Mother and Father; Well, I am in England, and only twenty miles from France, but even so, I shall not be satisfied until I get there and see a bit of the fun, and get back. That will be a happy day. Oh! By the way, I intend to send my ring home. If I do not some German will take it from me — if he can. Say, if I come back with a little Belgium girl don't be surprised, for they are a pretty lot and this place — Folkestone — has lots of them.*

Mother, dear, fry me two eggs, and prepare toast and coffee. Goodbye. Love and kisses to all.

Charlie"

THE CANADIANS ARE HOLDING THEIR OWN AT SANDLING CAMP

Over here! No further explanation needed!

The official view, however, of fraternisation between the troops and local girls seems to have reflected the social attitudes of the time. In his book, Folkestone During the War 1914-1919, Reverend J.C.Carlisle deals with the subject in these terms:

> The men were living under strange conditions. Life in Camp, thousands of miles away from home, was abnormal, and offered peculiar temptations. Men, feeling terribly lonely and hungry for companionship, with plenty of leisure time in a town of strangers, were confronted by attractions never experienced in their Homeland. They might easily have slipped into undesirable ways, and fallen victims to the Camp followers and to the worst phases of English social life, but for the good influences of the Chaplains and the attractions of the Hut."

With this puritanical assessment we can compare that written by Councillor John Jones in his book, Folkestone and the War:

Canadians and "Free Love"
Canadian heroes and British warriors, especially the

junior section, looked with merry eye upon the feminine heroines of Folkestone. Like the busmen of old, they adopted the motto, "None but the brave deserve the fair," and the fair reciprocated as only British damsels will. The gay promenades were visited very frequently, but secluded spots were also selected,--Lovers' Walks, Madeira Walk, the Sea-Shore where they could breathe sweet nothings in each others ears to the roar of the sea shells and to the ripple of the waves, and, while winning the War, these certain sections of Folkestone were happy. But alas! In war times, as in peace times, happiness is not always permanent. The course of love, whether true or illicit has its obstacles. The terrible Mrs. Grundy arrived and other forbidding personages of the Social Purity League."

Apparently, Mrs Grundy was unimpressed with the efforts of Folkestone's constabulary to curtail activities in some of the more secluded spots in the town and she proposed Women Police to root out these practices. In the event, true love seems to have triumphed over Mrs. Grundy and her followers; some 1100 local maidens sailed off to Canada with their soldier husbands.

Roll Up! Roll Up! Advertising two events at Radnor Park in Folkestone, both hosted by the Canadians.

In an echo of times past, the Canadian troops were quick to show off their musical, sporting and martial skills to the local townsfolk. Being superb horsemen, the gymkhanas hosted by the Canadian Mounted Rifles at Radnor Park were popular. Lieutenant Bertran was loudly cheered after his horse had fallen with him underneath but, undaunted, he extricated himself, vaulted on to another horse and rode off to finish the race. In an age when the cavalry charge was still thought to be a military option on the field of battle, the men enjoyed tent-pegging. In the event, the cavalry played little part in the Great War; the stalemate of the trenches and the horrors of No Man's Land were not going to succumb to the lance or the sword.

The people of Hythe were also treated to displays of Canadian skill with regular events held on the Green. Perhaps one of the most memorable, and controversial, was the Baseball match between Canadian and American forces played one Sunday in the summer of 1918.[17] After strong protests from the local Sunday observance supporters who condemned this 'Sunday desecration', the game went ahead and

[17] The Americans arrived in the area in some force during 1918.

was played in front of a crowd of 2000 spectators. The match was opened with the Mayor of Hythe, Councillor W.R.Cobay, pitching the first ball after which the Canadians went on to take the honours by 8 runs to 5.

The musical entertainments ranged from the Massed Bands of the 6th Infantry Brigade performing at Radnor Park on Dominion Day to providing the music at Christmas services at local churches; the Band of the 11th Battalion, CEF, did so in 1915 at the Radnor Park Congregational Church. A packed church heartily joined in with traditional carols, and was enthralled by solos from Sergeant Self who, in peacetime, had been a member of the Mendelssohn Choir in Toronto. During the spring and summer the Canadian musicians regularly performed at the bandstands on the Leas, as Captain James Evans described in a letter home to his wife: *"Shorncliffe. May 10, 1915. My own darling girl, Yesterday afternoon three of us officers went to the Leas and heard a Band concert by the Band of the 9th Reserve Cavalry it was lovely, after that we had tea at the Grand Hotel and more music by the Orchestra and then to the Parish Church in the evening, beautiful singing by a boys' choir."* Captain Evans was in the 32nd Battalion and he had been at Shorncliffe some years before when he had been discharged at the end of the Boer War. He wrote many letters home to his wife describing his time in Folkestone and whilst training at the School of Musketry in Hythe. In one letter he described his day in detail, *"School of Musketry, Hythe, Kent 14.6.15 My Darling Girl, Well sweetheart you want to know what my daily routine is, well will try and tell you what it has been while down at Hythe. At 7am my servant comes into the bedroom, puts out a hip bath, and warm water in hot water can, lays out my clothes, pulls up the blinds tells me it's 7 o'clock and goes out, takes me from 20 to 30 minutes to make up my mind to get up, after which I have a bath and shave and go to the mess for breakfast. At 9 o'clock there is a lecture in a sort of a school building. . . "*, He then relates the day's teaching schedule and continues, *". . .my dearest girl, so that gives you a fair idea of our routine at Hythe, Saturday afternoons is a holiday I generally go up to Risborough Barracks and stay until Sunday night. I and the two Waller boys took a row up the Canal which goes through Hythe it is very pretty. . ."* After his training at the School of Musketry, Captain

Time to Relax. Photo taken by Captain James Evans of two friends boating on the Royal Military Canal, Hythe.

Evans was designated an Instructor and, instead of being sent to the Front, he taught the new arrivals of the Second Contingent, something that causes him some disquiet, as he explained to his wife, *"Risborough, Shorncliffe 27.7.15 My darling girl, . . .I'm too busy just now, training these men in Musketry and furthermore I don't care to be going among all my old friends again without having been at the front. . . Major Dyer went back to the front two days ago, that's what I consider rotten, officers getting over their wounds are sent back, and we who have not been over are kept for instructional purposes."* Most of James Evans' letters home are light-hearted and

Airship at Capel. From an original watercolour dated 1914 and signed 'Goddard', this airship flies majestically over the coast with Capel le Ferne and the RNAS station in the background.

reassuring, as though he does not want to worry his wife that, in reality, he is in the middle of a war and that Folkestone is very much in the front line. Louis Duff of the 28th (North Western) Battalion, in a letter to his aunt and uncle in Saskatchewan, is less reticent: *"29th June 1915, Dibgate Camp, Shorncliffe: Just a line to let you know we arrived OK and am well... We have two pretty coast towns close by, Hythe west of us an hours walk and Folkestone, a popular seaside resort, east of us...On a clear day France shows up plainly. Submarines and Torpedo Boat Destroyers are patrolling the sea all the time. Aeroplanes and dirigibles are a common sight."* Duff's reference to dirigibles is interesting; they were constantly in action over the Channel keeping safe the troopships between Folkestone and Boulogne. The Royal Navy ships of the Dover Patrol were accompanied by airships, some free-flying, others tethered to the warships, and capable of spotting and dropping depth charges on enemy submarines. The airships were kept in huge hangars on the cliff tops at Capel Le Ferne, to the east of Folkestone, on ground adjacent to the Royal Oak, with out stations at Hythe and Lydd. The four canvas hangars for the Hythe balloons were erected on land near to the lifeboat station at the end of St Leonards Road. The success of the Dover Patrol and its escort of airships was astonishing; over the four years of the war there were 10,686 crossings between Folkestone and Boulogne and nearly 11 million troops were carried. Not a single soldier was lost due to enemy action whilst crossing the Channel, despite many attempts by the Germans to disrupt this vital artery.

For those waiting to embark for the Front, the ominous rumble of war drifted across the Channel, as recorded by Lieutenant S.C.Kirkland, who was camped at West Sandling, *"When there is a heavy bombardment on around Zeebruge or at the west of the battle line at Dunkirk, or in the direction of Ypres, we can distinctly hear the rumble of the big guns...I thought at first the noise I heard was thunder but as I was hearing it every morning I made enquiries and was told it was the noise of battle."* So close was Folkestone to the front lines that it was the case that a soldier could eat his breakfast in Folkestone and be fighting in the trenches by lunchtime.

The journey to the Front was not always a smooth operation. Although the Dover Patrol and the airships ensured the safety of transports on the crossing between Folkestone and Boulogne, there were occasional obstacles much closer to home. Following the Royal inspection on

Off to the Front. With their full kit bags and the sun shining, these men cheerfully make their way along the Leas towards the harbour. Did they have any idea of the horrors that awaited them?

the 2nd September, 1915, preparations were made for the Second Contingent to transfer to France. The official history of the Canadian 28th Battalion describes the attempt to march from Shorncliffe to Folkestone Harbour,

Early September 1915: 28th Battalion received a warning order: prepare to move to France. Major General Turner takes command of 2nd Division from General Steele, who remains to command the training camp at Shorncliffe. The Battalion is issued British uniforms, boots, webbing, equipment, all of it new and stiff. This, along with the issued ammunition was quite a load, men's packs were 90 pounds, officers 75 pounds.

September 16, 1915: The event called 'The Retreat from Moscow' by the 28th Battalion. The Battalion received orders to embark for France. The march to embark at Folkstone is diverted onto narrow, dusty side roads for security reasons. High temperatures, high humidity, tall hedges, new webbing & new boots resulted in sore feet, severe chaffing, exhaustion and confusion. Some troops dropped out on the 10-mile march. Sailing was postponed due to reports of submarines in the English Channel so a bivouac was arranged on St. Martin's Plain, one mile from the port. The local guide became lost, leading most of the battalion on a 5-mile trek. Stragglers and separated parties began to fall out and lie down on sidewalks, porches & half a company at the railroad station. Colonel Embury was found to be quite embarrassed that a fit, well-trained outfit could fall apart so easily. Major Alex Ross gathered the stragglers onto the plain in the early morning. The bivouac was poor as the water supply was limited and all supplies (including food & cookers) were already loaded on the ship.

September 17, 1915 - A night march from St. Martin's Plain to Folkstone harbour takes 1/2 hour. There are none of the incidents of the previous day's march. The Battalion embarks for France.

Quick March. More troops heading along the Leas, destined for the Western Front. The bandstand can be seen in the background.

Private Donald Fraser, whose views on the adequacy of the training have already been noted, described the incident in his journal in his forthright way,

> Friday, September 17, 1915: Anyway, our training was at an end, word was passed around that we were leaving today for France. The camp was all excitement. At last we were to witness real fighting. It was almost too good to be true. Everyone was pleased at the idea though a bit dubious of the outcome. The consequences, however, were thrown to the winds, the only thing that mattered was we were bound for France. Orders to strike camp were given and in due time we were on the move, our packs choke full of clothing, etc. It was a memorable day as our brigade stepped out on the road and marched for Folkestone through Lympne, Hythe, Seabrook and Sandgate. The march was gruelling one. Our packs were so heavy that the strappings almost cut into the flesh and there were many connivances employed to ease the aching back, and shoulders. Near Folkestone at the Leas we halted and lay on the road. By this time the stragglers had caught up. It soon became evident that there was something wrong and everyone was enquiring the reason for the delay. The command rang out along the lines, "about turn," then we learned the reason - there were mines in the English Channel and we could not cross until the sweepers announced all clear. Our first battle, the retreat from Folkestone, commenced. Twos and threes were falling out by the roadside, the climb to the plains above Sandgate took the heart out of many, so they took up their abode for the night on the roadside, in gardens, in the fields, amidst bushes, and a few fortunate ones managed into houses. The Companies got badly mixed. By the time a halt was called the battalion was widely scattered. About a couple of dozen, including the writer, represented 'A' Company. That night we slept on [Sir John Moore's] Plains under the canopy of heaven with only what we carried with us for covering. Next morning and forenoon the stragglers began to arrive from all directions and by the afternoon we were up to strength again..."
>
> "Saturday, September 18, 1915: The channel was evidently clear for in the early evening we were on the road again. At Folkestone we embarked. The British Navy had its

sentinels out, one particular vessel keeping a watchful eye on us. It darted hither and thither, racing alongside us or crossing our bow or stern. In the fading light England was soon lost to view - to many forever.

Soldiers in Hythe c1914. Late afternoon (note the shadows) and these men are returning to Shorncliffe after a hot day on the Ranges. They are passing a charabanc outside the cafe, with the Red Lion next door. In the background is an unhorsed tram waiting to go into the shed.

Of course, the ships sailing from Folkestone to Boulogne, full with fresh troops on their way to the front, were not empty on the return journey; there were the wounded to bring home. The first of these landed at Folkestone harbour only three weeks after the outbreak of war. It was perhaps a reflection of the belief that the war would be short-lived that led to an almost carnival atmosphere reported in the Folkestone Herald:

BRITISH WOUNDED
Landed at Folkestone
In Shorncliffe Hospital

The first British wounded to be brought back to this country from the front were landed at Folkestone Harbour from Boulogne on Thursday and their arrival aroused great interest and excitement.

The soldiers were conveyed in motor cars through the town to the Camp, being enthusiastically greeted by the crowds in the streets. Most of the men appeared to be slightly wounded and were able to walk with assistance. They displayed great cheerfulness.

As 1914 gave way to a new year, it brought with it the full horrors of the conflict; names such as Ypres, Loos, Neuve Chapelle and Hill 60 would come to represent the monuments of experience upon which the innocence of a generation was sacrificed. In 1916 it was the Somme with Arras and Passchendaele the following year; these and a host of other places were to become as potent in the nation's consciousness as

Canadian War Contingent Association.

Queen's Canadian Military Hospital.   Beachborough Park, Shorncliffe, Kent.

Beachborough House. This large mansion house was taken over as a hospital during WWI, initially for Belgian wounded and then by the Canadians.

Agincourt and Crecy. The optimism and air of adventure of the early days of the war gave way to the dark reality of weekly newspaper columns, listing Folkestone and Hythe's sons and husbands killed or missing. The wounded continued to arrive at Folkestone harbour in increasing numbers, from where they were despatched to hospitals in London and across the south-east. Canadian casualties were treated at hospitals in and around Folkestone. The ever increasing numbers of casualties led to hotels, convalescent homes and other suitable establishments being pressed into service and converted to hospitals for the men. At the outbreak of the war the gleaming white mansion of Beachborough, a pre-war haunt of David Lloyd George, had been thrown open to wounded Belgian soldiers and by 1915 it had become The Queen's Canadian Military Hospital. For many Canadians who recovered there the abiding memory was the symmetrical Beachborough Hill topped by a summer house built, legend recalled, by one of the 18th century Brockmans who had a weakness for bad language, and who took himself to his hilltop retreat where his outbursts would not cause offence. In May 1916 a reporter from the Folkestone and Hythe Herald went to Beachborough to visit the wounded from the First Battle of Ypres. One of the lads he spoke to was Private E. Edwards from Ontario who had been shot twice and who gave an account of the fighting, *"It was a terrible stew, and I don't mind if I don't go*

West Cliff Hotel, Folkestone. During WWI the hotel was used as a hospital, specialising in facial surgery and nicknamed 'the nose factory'. Later renamed Majestic Hotel, the site is now occupied by shops and a Chinese restaurant.

through such a time again. The losses on both sides were something terrific. We severely punished the Germans, but many a bullet from their guns found its mark on our side." Shorncliffe Military Hospital was renamed No. 9 Canadian General Hospital and, in common with the other medical facilities, was staffed principally by Canadian doctors and nurses. The West Cliff Hotel was turned into a hospital and became known as 'the nose factory' for its pioneering work on the faces of soldiers who had suffered facial injuries. Around Folkestone numerous pre-war nursing and convalescent homes were converted for use as hospitals and rest homes for the soldiers; of these the most notable was the Bevan Hospital on Sandgate sea front. At the turn of the century it was known as Beach Rocks Convalescent Home and it was here, in 1900, that the wounded from the Boer War were received. The premises had subsequently fallen into disuse and, by 1914, were in a dilapidated state. It was

Staff of the Bevan, Sandgate. Doctors, nurses and helpers, together with their two dogs, of the famous WWI hospital and convalescent home at Sandgate.

at this point that the redoubtable Miss M.A. Mumford, with the help of the Voluntary Aid Detachment (Kent 30), took the building over and converted it into one of the most comfortable hospitals on the south-east coast. By the end of the war over 12,000 patients had passed through the Bevan and it had acquired a reputation for wholesome cooking and, because of its open-air courtyard and homely atmosphere, for curing the worst cases of sepsis.

The war continued through 1916 and into 1917 and the people of Folkestone and Hythe had all but forgotten the halcyon days of pre-war gentility. Roads had been churned up by thousands of army boots and military vehicles, civic gardens were left untended, and the buildings looked drab and neglected. Life had settled into its own rhythm with soldiers coming and going, with women taking over the jobs vacated by the men who were fighting, injured or dead. Despite being so near to the front the local towns and military camps were not in the firing line. Early in the conflict there had been worries about attacks from Zeppelins which made regular sorties across the Channel but, apart from a raid on Otterpool Camp near Lympne in October 1915, in which fourteen Canadian artillerymen were killed, and another occasion when bombs were dropped on Romney Marsh, these did not materialise. The shelling suffered at the hands of the German navy by a number of coastal towns never hit Folkestone or Hythe. On Friday the 25th May 1917 everything changed. Although it was nearly 6pm, many shops in Tontine Street were still open. It would be Whitsun Bank Holiday on the Monday, and there was still a brisk trade with wives buying extra provisions for the long weekend. Quite a queue had formed at Stokes the greengrocers, while mothers chatted and their children played nearby. At Shorncliffe Camp the troops, mostly Canadians, were returning after a day's training. There then came the sound of aeroplane engines. Initial thoughts that 'they're ours' turned to terror as bombs started to fall. The squadron of German Gotha bombers had approached from the west, attacking Hythe and Sandgate and then the army camps before swooping over Folkestone town centre where the majority of their high explosive bombs were dropped. The attack was the most devastating of the war and it cut a swathe of death and destruction. The worst of the casualties were in Tontine Street where 60 men women and children were killed instantly with many more dying of their injuries and nearly a hundred more were seriously injured. At Shorncliffe camp 18 soldiers, of whom 16 were Canadians, were killed outright, with a further 90 injured, including 86 Canadians. One of those to receive only minor injury was Konnie Johannsen from Winnipeg. He had joined the 223rd Overseas (XI Reserve) Battalion in 1916 and had arrived at Shorncliffe just two weeks before the Raid. Konnie kept a diary of his wartime experiences and here describes that dreadful day,

Florence Rumsey. Aged 17 at the time of the Air Raid Florrie, as she was known, died the day after from her wounds. She was a bookkeeper at Stokes Brothers in Tontine Street where the death toll was greatest.

Friday May 25th: Slept until 10. Got up and Tubs told us to get ready to move from Lower Dibgate to 11th. Arrived 11th at noon. Ate under shade of trees by road through 11th and 8th. Moved into quarantine tent and had just fixed up tent and finished our supper when 'Fritzers' raided us. One bomb dropped 15ft from us. Bill E, Bill, Tom, Hank, Davey and I all cut by flying glass. Raid lasted about an hour. Bill E and I hit for prairies and big oak tree. Helped girls over fence on way. Town of Folkestone, 2 streets blown to pieces. Holes out through our tent from Shrapnel. Left for Hospital 8.30 for anti-poison injection. Assisted carrying the wounded at Hospital. Had lunch at 11.30 (pm) there and then walked back to our tent. Could not go to sleep for a long time.

After the Great Raid[18] there were recriminations; why was there no warning, where were the defences? In response anti-aircraft guns were installed in Cherry Garden Avenue and Earls Avenue, together with warning sirens, searchlights and shelters. Despite many air raid warnings in the months that followed the raid there were no further attacks, but the people of Folkestone lived in constant fear and, for many, the only answer was to leave the town for the duration. Many of the victims of the

The Great Air Raid. Showing the remains of Stokes' Brothers greengrocers in Tontine Street after the attack on 25th May 1917.

[18] See Appendix J for a full list of fatalities following the Great Air Raid.

Victory Parade. A procession of soldiers, sailors, nurses and, bringing up the rear, two ambulances, marching through Folkestone in 1919. The rear of the procession is passing what today is Debenhams. Note the American flags. The Canadians fought under the Union Flag.

attack were buried in a joint service at the Cheriton Road cemetery, followed by a memorial service on the 3rd June 1917, led by the Archbishop of Canterbury. His words may have provided some comfort for those who had lost family and friends in the devastating attack, *"We in this corner of England on this Kentish coast have the solemn privilege of being the bit of England nearest the enemy. Some people must be in the forefront and, so far as English soil is concerned, the people to whom that special trust is given are those living at Folkestone . . . , and we mean to be worthy of it."* The people did rally and the stoicism for which this generation is rightly remembered carried them through.

With the end of the war in November 1918 it was time to count the cost, but first there were the celebrations. Hythe's wartime mayor, William Cobay, gave a tea party for 350 returning servicemen, church bells rang out and 1,100 children were presented with bronze medals inscribed with a dove on one side and the inscription, "To commemorate the victorious conclusion of the Great War 1914-1919", on the other. In Folkestone, the celebrations were followed by the realisation that things had changed

Victory Party, Folkestone. This photo was taken in Dover Street. The faces reveal a mixture of joy and disbelief but, most of all, simple weariness after having endured four years of conflict.

'Demob'. Issued with their rations, these men are on their way home. Folkestone was one of a dozen national demob centres. This picture was taken in Marine Terrace.

forever; the days of concerts and fashion shows on the Leas, of wealthy holidaymakers, catered for by low paid domestic staff, were consigned to history. If it was to survive, the town would need to attract a new clientele, the day trippers and the new middle classes on their annual holidays. For the soldiers returning to 'a land fit for heroes' there began the process of demobilisation. Around the country a dozen demob' centres were set up, with Shorncliffe being one of the main sites, processing up to 7000 men each day as they arrived from France. The procedure became a production line; the men would move from one table to the next receiving in turn £2 on account of pay, then a Protection Certificate and unemployment policy, next their rations and finally a free railway ticket to their home station. Because the men were returning in far greater numbers than could be processed, a backlog built up and the rest camps were crowded with those who had been away from home, sometimes for several years. In early 1919, the patience of the men was pushed to the limit and there was a demonstration by 10,000 of them in Folkestone against the slow progress. For the Canadians the demobilisation arrangements were even more complex, but even their journey home would begin

Farewell from the Canadians. Before leaving for home, the Canadian Army presented 8 stained glass windows to Shorncliffe Station. This one depicts the Mapleleaf in the lower panel. Others showed the white horse of Kent, Invicta. The windows were removed in 1964 and are now stored at the National Railway Museum in York.

with a train from Shorncliffe Station[19]. For soldiers over the years the station had been the first or last they had seen of England and for the Canadians bound for home there must have been many emotional farewells. The symbolism of Shorncliffe Station to these men was clearly demonstrated with the presentation by the Canadian army of eight stained glass windows which were installed in the station building; unfortunately they have long been replaced by plain glass or the windows simply boarded up. There remain, of course, the War Memorials in our towns where the annual act of remembrance takes place. Not so well known, perhaps, is the cairn sitting at the roadside at the top of the Road of Remembrance in Folkestone. It simply records,

ROAD OF REMEMBRANCE
During the Great War tens of thousands of
British soldiers passed along this road on their way
to and from the front in Europe

To this inscription we can acknowledge that it was not just British soldiers who passed that way; men from across the British Empire and beyond marched to the harbour and then to the Western Front. Not all returned. Of every nine who went to fight, one did not come home, and another two were wounded.

The final word in this story is left to Private Charles Davies from Winnipeg, who had served in the 12 Canadian Field Ambulance. The following lines appeared in a Canadian newspaper in 1919, though apparently written from the front. They could, perhaps, have been written by any one of the tens of thousands of soldiers who served at Shorncliffe over the previous century:

SHORNCLIFFE CAMP
Folkestone, thou Queen of the Southern Coast,
I'm loath to leave your grassy warren;
Those steep white cliffs that beacon like a genial host
Receding from my eyes nigh dim with tears.
What soothing hours and happy days so dear does memory recall;
The walk along the Leas, the leafy undercliff, and Oh, that changing sea,
When the rich red sunset sparkles on thy face,
Such are my thoughts of thee picture of grace.

Garden of England! Brave Men of Kent!
Think of your heritage: the flowers sweet scent,
That wooded glade at Seabrook, primrose clad;
The glimpse of moving picture shore to make you glad.

[19] Not all Canadians returned to Canada. See Appendix I, 'A Soldier's Tale'.

Those verdant meads of Shorncliffe Plain,
Bright green as emeralds after rain.
Deep down in mist of blue lies sleeping Sandgate town,
Whose twinkling lights shine like some fairy's crown.

St. Martin's spire, neath which brave Plimsol sleeps,
Whose noble work the British sailor reaps;
The bugle blasts and all war's grim array,
Much as it did in Moore's far distant day.

Not even the mists of Passchendaele and its blood strewn
duckboard track
Can blot from out my memory the charm of Radnor Park.
Who would not fight for thee, dear land,
For every flower and Kentish maid's fair hand.

Who cares for the muddy trenches and the shrapnel's
piercing scream,
The waves of poison and all the ghastly scene?
There are those away in the Golden West dearer than
Nelson's name-
Mothers and wives and sisters; it's for them we play the
game.

Chapter 9

SHORNCLIFFE MILITARY CEMETERY

Very few cemeteries, military or civilian, can provide such a peaceful or picturesque atmosphere as Shorncliffe Military Cemetery. It is perched on a south west facing escarpment giving dramatic views across the rolling hills of Kent which draw the eye across the sweep of Hythe Bay to the plains of the Romney Marsh. On a summer's day the sun can blaze down, leading the visitor to seek shade under one of the tall pine trees which fringe the site whilst, in winter, the Channel gales bellow up the hillside as an accompaniment to the thundering seas below. The cemetery is a reminder that, throughout history, men and women who are called to the Colours are all too often asked to make the supreme sacrifice; but not all who rest

at Shorncliffe died in action. There are wives, children, retired soldiers and civilian workers. There are soldiers from Canada, Belgium, Portugal and Poland and six members of the Chinese Labour Corps. In a true reflection of the history of the nearby camp, practically every regiment in the British army, past and present, is

Shorncliffe Military Cemetery, Folkestone. With views to the west over Hythe Bay, the cemetery occupies the most beautiful and tranquil spot.

represented there, some of them lying alongside men of the Royal Air Force, the Police, Merchant Navy and Coastguard[20].

It is not known how long the military cemetery has occupied its present spot. The first recorded burial at Shorncliffe cemetery is of Private George Burrows of the 6th Inniskilling Dragoons on the 28th August 1856, a victim of the Crimean War. This poses a question: where are the remains of all those soldiers who died before Private Burrows? The original graveyard was situated in the rough-cut sloping ground to the left and right of the top entrance to the present cemetery. Property records reveal that the Trustees of the Reverend William Brockman sold this land to the Board of Ordnance in 1872 for the sum of £160. Had the Reverend already

[20] See Appendix L for a list of Regiments represented at the cemetery.

allowed the land to be used as a burial ground before he sold it to the military? This certainly appears to be the case from the burial of Private Burrows and many others recorded in the Shorncliffe Cemetery Burial Register. Consequently, there may be many more soldiers buried at the site, dating back well before 1858. It is a fact that the authorities at Shorncliffe believe that the original graveyard is full, and that most of the original graves would have been marked with wooden crosses which have long since perished. This is borne out by a report appearing in The Illustrated London News of the 16th July 1859, which describes the graveyard,

> The churchyard is picturesquely situated on the spur of a hill which runs out into the romantic-looking valley of Seabrook. Here traces may be seen of the Foreign Legion, for which this camp was originally erected, in the wooden and stone crosses placed at the head of some of the graves.

But these observations only take us back as far as the 1850s; surely there was a burial ground at the time of Sir John Moore's command at Shorncliffe during the early years of the nineteenth century? In fact, from the recollections of William Surtees of the 95th Rifles, whom we met in Chapter 1, it is clear that there was. He recounts an incident in 1804,

> A short while before my appointment as sergeant, a most melancholy occurrence took place in the vicinity of our cantonment. A large Dutch East Indiaman, outward bound to Batavia, and full of troops, in passing the channel, mistook, I understand, the light at Dungeness for one on the French coast, and in consequence stood in towards Dymchurch wall instead of keeping out to sea. As might be expected she was not long in striking on the wall, running with her bow quite close under the road, and in an instant, almost, went to pieces; and although numbers of people were early on the spot, and some, I believe, at the very moment she struck, they could render the unfortunate sufferers no effectual aid, although only a few yards distant from them. Out of about 800 persons on board, only seven men were saved. Many poor fellows, I understand, attempted to swim on the shore, some on planks, and others without any aid; but such was the tremendous swell, and the general destruction of the ship so rapid, that only those seven before mentioned succeeded; and they were not without being all more or less injured by pieces of the wreck. An admiral, I

ground had been specially used at the time of an epidemic, but the evidence seems to indicate that it was generally used for the Castle Garrison interments.

The obelisk gives a number of interesting details about the history of the graves and how they now come to be at Shorncliffe.

The Canadian Graves

In answer to England's call for help at the outbreak of the First World War Canada recruited many thousands of her young men. They received training at home before sailing for England. The Canadian Expeditionary Force spent the summer of 1915 training at Shorncliffe before leaving for the front in September. Many did not return; the wounded who did were treated at the military hospital at Shorncliffe, but the skill and dedication of the doctors and nurses, most of whom were also Canadian, were not always enough. Private Arthur Chesnut from Orilla, Ontario, was wounded in France in August 1916 and then evacuated back to the Canadian Military Hospital at Shorncliffe, but he succumbed to his wounds on the 5th September and was buried at Shorncliffe Cemetery.

Not all of the Canadian soldiers buried at Shorncliffe died as a result of wounds received at the front. William Meehan was 36 years old when he volunteered in 1915. He had served in his local militia in New Brunswick for the past ten years and he answered his country's call to arms despite the pleas of his wife, Alice, and their three young children. Private Meehan was assigned to the 23rd Infantry Battalion and sailed for England with the rest of the Canadian Second Contingent in spring 1915. Sadly, William succumbed to meningitis soon after his arrival at the barracks on Dibgate Plain and, although transferred from Shorncliffe Military Hospital to Folkestone Isolation Hospital on the 14th August, he died from the disease three days later and was buried at the Military Cemetery (Plot N.288). Fittingly, the rolling hills of the cemetery, with the sea as a backdrop bear a striking similarity to William's birthplace in St. John, New Brunswick.

William Meehan's wedding. This picture records the wedding of William Meehan to Alice Whitlock in York County, New Brunswick on 8th April 1901. William joined the Canadian Army in WWI, but died soon after his arrival at Shorncliffe and is buried in the cemetery.

A number of the Canadians who lie at Shorncliffe were victims of the Great Raid on the 25th May 1917, when German aircraft bombed the camp and nearby towns. One of the soldiers to die when the bombs fell on Shorncliffe camp was Oron Alfred Jenner. He was the only son of Elizabeth Jenner from Toronto and had only arrived in England four weeks earlier to join the 3rd Reserve Battalion as Company Quarter Master Sergeant. Oron was 26 when he died.

Canadian Flower Day at Shorncliffe Cemetery. The children in this 1930s photograph are performing an act or remembrance which has taken place annually since the end of the Great War.

Canada Day 2003. The Memorial service in 2003. For some of these children, the tribute was first undertaken by their parents and grandparents.

Two hundred and ninety-six Canadian soldiers are buried at Shorncliffe and on Canada Day each year a Remembrance Service, originally called Canadian Flower Day, is held attended by local dignitaries, representatives from the Canadian High Commission, and the Canadian Veterans Association, together with the local British Army Command, and the British Legion. With a brief interruption during the Second World War, this ceremony has taken place every year since 1917. The ceremony has a poignancy and uniqueness from the tradition that children from local schools attend; each child stands by an individual Canadian headstone holding a spray of flowers which is then placed on the grave. Some children today are repeating an act of remembrance that their parents and grandparents performed when they were children.

It was a cruel coincidence of timing that the idea for the very first Canadian Flower Day was published in the Hythe Reporter by Edward Palmer, its founding editor, on the day following that horrific air raid in May 1917.

'For Valour'

Buried at Shorncliffe Military Cemetery are three recipients of the highest award for bravery – the Victoria Cross.

Bombardier Joseph Charles Brennan, Royal Artillery

Joseph Brennan was born at St Probus near Truro in Cornwall in August 1836. He was serving with the Royal Artillery during the Indian Mutiny when he won his Victoria Cross, and his citation records:

For marked gallantry at the assault on the 3rd April, 1858, in bringing up two guns of the Hyderabad Contingent, manned by natives, laying each under a heavy fire from the walls, and directing them so accurately as to compel the enemy to abandon his battery.

An interesting historical postscript is that a woman, Rani Lakshmi Bai, who had been proclaimed ruler of Jhansi in 1852, led the Indian forces at the time. She was killed in action a few weeks after the action of April 1858.

Joseph Brennan, who was promoted to Sergeant, died of pneumonia on the 24th September 1872 whilst serving with the 1st Brigade Royal Artillery at Shorncliffe. His original grave seems to have been unmarked, but in 1995 a headstone was unveiled at a service of dedication led by the Master Gunner, General Sir Martin Farndale KCB.

Bombardier Joseph Brennan VC. Awarded the VC for his actions during the Indian Mutiny in 1858.

Private Patrick McHale, Northumberland Fusiliers

According to the St. George's Gazette[21] of the 30th April 1894 Pat McHale joined the Fusiliers on the 18th December 1847 at Parkhurst Barracks on the Isle of Wight when he was 21 years old. He was a most powerful man, standing six feet two inches tall with sandy hair and a fair complexion, his face covered in freckles. McHale served for 9 years in Mauritius before his regiment sailed for India in 1857 to help quell the Mutiny there. There he fought in several battles distinguishing himself as a formidable close combat soldier. It was at Cawnpore that he won his VC, and his citation reads:

This 6ft 2in Irishman was born in 1826 and enlisted in the 5th Fusiliers on December 18th 1847 at the age of 21. This Irishman's favourite weapon was the bayonet, and his hobby capturing Sepoy artillerymen. On more than one occasion during the relief and the following siege of the residency, he was well to the fore in bayoneting Sepoy gunners.

Further details were given of the action:

The 5th were ordered to storm the Cawnpore Battery which they did in their usual style. As the storming party rushed the battery the first to enter was the gallant Captain L'Estrange of Arrah fame. He was shot instantly. McHale who was at his heels forgot his bayonet exercise and used the butt end of his heavy Enfield rifle so effectively that by the time the remainder of the Company got in the Pandies were convinced it was time to go.

Away they ran for their lives shouting that there was a red haired devil in the Battery killing them all.

Private Patrick McHale VC. It is clear from this picture that McHale was an imposing figure; with his bayonet presented he was probably terrifying! He won his VC at Cawnpore.

It was whilst at Shorncliffe that, on the 26th October 1866, Private 2626 Pat McHale died of heart failure. He was forty years of age.

Private John Doogan, Kings Dragoon Guards

When he died in January 1940, John Doogan VC had reached the grand age of 86.

---

[21] See Appendix K for the full text of the article published in the St George's Gazette.

He had survived the First Boer War, having been wounded, and re-enlisted at the start of the First World War as a recruiting sergeant, enduring the death of two sons, Jack and Dick in that war. He lived long enough to witness the outbreak of the Second World War.

Private Doogan won his Victoria Cross during an assault on Laing's Neck on the 28th January 1881. His citation records:

Private Doogan, servant to Major W V Brownlow, was charging with his troop, when Major Brownlow's horse was shot. Seeing the major dismounted among the Boers, he rode up, and though himself severely wounded, dismounted and wished Major Brownlow to take his horse, receiving another wound while trying to get him to take it.

Trooper Doogan in action. From a painting by the Victorian artist, Harry Payne. Here Doogan is rescuing Major Brownlow during the Transvaal War in 1881.

Regimental records give further details of the action:

The mounted squadron moving on the right of the infantry gradually drew up the slope of the isolated hill on our right and, coming under fire of the Boers on the hill, faced the hill and charged. This charge was splendidly led by Major Brownlow who, with Sergeant Major Lunny, Kings Dragoon Guards, was first on the ridge. Major Brownlow's horse was shot under him and Sergeant Major Lunny was instantly killed; but Major Brownlow shot the Boer leader with his revolver, and continued to lead his men, who now crowned the ridge. Could he have been promptly supported, the hill was won, for the Boers had already begun to retreat; but the fire was still heavy, while many of the horses were quite untrained to stand fire. The support was checked; the leading troop fatigued with all the leaders down, could not push on, and the whole gave way down the hill.

Upon his return to England, John Doogan was hospitalised at the military hospital at Netley near Southampton. Here he met local lass, Mary Evans, who was

Trooper John Doogan VC. Doogan lived in Folkestone until his death in 1940. His gravestone at Shorncliffe Cemetery records that he lost two sons in WWI.

a nurse. They married and moved back to his home at Welshpool. After Mary's death Doogan married his housemaid but it turned out that she was already married and that marriage was therefore dissolved. A proud man, Doogan would often be seen marching down the main street with his VC pinned to his waistcoat. Then, when he was 72 years of age, the old soldier married again. His wife was a girl of just twenty and they were ostracised in their home town and so moved to Folkestone where Doogan had sisters. They lived at 5, Tilley Road and, until his death, he regularly attended meetings of the Folkestone and District branch of the South African War Veterans Association.

The Cemetery Today

Shorncliffe Military Cemetery continues to be used for burials and the visitor will see many graves continue to be marked with fresh flowers. It is not unusual to spot a couple of old soldiers sitting in the sun on a summer's day, remembering old comrades and old campaigns. Care of the Cemetery is shared between the Commonwealth War Graves Commission and the Shorncliffe authorities. In January 2004, during a comprehensive replanting by the CWGC, a number of unmarked graves were discovered. These are thought to be the burial sites of 15 children who died during the early 1900s.

The Headstone of John Doogan VC. Recording that his sons, Jack and Dick, were killed in the Great War, and his wife, Mary, had died in 1924.

APPENDIX A

List of Ships built and Commissioned at Sandgate

Date	Name	Type/No of Guns	Tonnes
1771	Serpent	Sloop/14	314
1782	Pluto	Sloop/16	426
1783	Rattler	Sloop/16	341
1783	Kate	6th Rate/28	594
1784	Circe	6th Rate/28	594
1784	Hussar	6th Rate/28	597
1784	Dido	6th Rate/28	595
1784	Brisk	Sloop/16	340
1785	Rose	6th Rate/28	596
1787	Alligator	6th Rate/28	599
1788		Sheerness tender	148
1810	Dwarf	Cutter/10	203

APPENDIX B

Instructions for Home Defence Published by the Adjutant General issued in February 1801. (As described by Col J.F.C. Fuller in 'Sir John Moore's System of Training')

Enemy's objective:

The invasion of this country, which may be accomplished on some one or more points of our extensive coasts, in order immediately to threaten the capital and centre of the kingdom.

Preliminary measures:

The commanding Generals were instructed to make themselves "thoroughly acquainted with the local situation in their districts," and to "frame a regular system of defence and operation, which they will communicate in its various degrees, and with full explanation to each person materially concerned with its execution. They will point out the most probable places of descent from an enemy, the works that now exist for their defence, and the arrangements to be made at each for opposing him."

They were to arrange for "hastening the inhabitants in the neighbourhood of the enemy to withdraw their cattle and horses, to enforce this by every means, and to destroy, without compunction, whatever provision is tardy in its removal or can be of use to him; such removals will be made to a sufficient distance, according to the district plan ascertained, and the routes in it ordered and pointed out. Such arrangements in consequence of the general plan must be made with the Lord

Lieutenants and Magistrates of the different counties as may ensure the punctual execution of these most essential services."

Clearance of Cattle;

"From the moment that an enemy is discovered from the coast and pointing to a place of landing, the driving of the country must begin, be strongly enforced and made, if possible, by other routes than those of the probable operation of the troops, whose movements must not be interrupted; and when the acting direction of the enemy is sufficiently ascertained, nothing within the probability of his reach should be suffered to remain; nor would this incommode the advanced troops, for their supplies would readily come up from their rear; and, above all, the removal of horses of every description must be accomplished. If this is rigidly executed, his future movements will become exceedingly slow and fatiguing, perhaps impossible. The mode of doing all this is prescribed, and will be arranged in every district of the exposed coast, the execution allotted to the yeoman cavalry, and every reasonable hope may be entertained of its being carried into effect.

"Nothing will more effectually disappoint and disconcert the project of an invading enemy than the driving and abandonment of the country, and the total destruction of the roads for miles round, whatever point he made his landing at, or at least for several miles on each side of the route he meant to pursue. Could this be accomplished as easily as imagined, he would find himself in a desert, unable to advance or to give the time necessary to free himself from the first embarrassments thrown in his way, and which would only be a prelude to more considerable opposition. This alone, persevered in, would stop all progress, his distresses and want would increase in proportion to his numbers, and if his communication was interrupted by a superior naval force, he must soon be reduced to the greatest difficulties. But as this cannot be expected to the desired amount, it may be desirable to point out how far the roads of the country should be destroyed, so as to be disadvantageous to the enemy and advantageous to ourselves."

First Defensive Steps:

Immediately information has been received that a landing at a certain place is imminent, "the troops will be cantoned or encamped in the manner that appears the most advantageous." The various lines of defence will be held, and the troops will hold themselves, "in a state of field preparation." The Generals commanding districts will further call out the Yeoman and Volunteer corps, and see that they carry out the duties allotted to them.

Action if the Enemy Advances:

"On the first landing of the enemy, if he cannot be prevented in the attempt, not a moment must be lost in assembling the troops, and pushing on the most advanced, however few in number, till more can be collected. The great object must be constantly to harass, alarm and tire the enemy, and to impede his progress, till a sufficient force assembles to attack him. The nature of the country affords every advantage for that purpose; intricate and enclosed, it is never to be lost sight of by the light troops, and every inch of the ground, every field may to a degree be disputed, even by inferior numbers. As soon as ever he has quitted the coast, he must be surrounded in front, flank, and rear; a knowledge of the country, and a superiority of cavalry gives the advantage, he must be obliged to fight for every article of sustenance. The country must be driven, and everything useful within his reach destroyed without mercy; this, the necessity of the case, and the infinite consequence of giving him an immediate check, demand; cattle and horses must at all events be removed."

Tactics of Delay:

"It is desirable to reduce the enemy to advance on a small front, to prevent him from extending his flanks, and to throw as many obstacles in the way of his progress to the front as can be devised; but to do this it is necessary to reserve access to his flanks, to be able to follow his rear and, in opposing him in front, to have our own rear open for a speedy retreat, or for receiving supplies and reinforcements…

"The great extent of our coast makes it difficult to guard it everywhere, and from the nature of an invasion an enemy, if he escapes our navy and all the perils of the sea, generally arrives with a force much superior to that which can be assembled to oppose him…" After resisting as much as possible, the troops should, on a given signal, quit the ground, and assemble again some half-mile farther back. "…When the enemy shall be master of the shore the troops are never to lose sight of him; they are to fall back to such a moderate distance as circumstances seem to require; they are to extend, and on arriving from all quarters to endeavour to encompass him, for their general intention and application must be to draw as much advantage from attacks on his flanks and rear as they can propose to do from opposition in front…these attacks should be kept up incessantly, made by bodies both of small and large numbers. And in acting in this manner the troops are to understand that, though our object or situation does induce us at first to fall back gradually till our force can be collected on a given point and enabled to advance upon and attack the enemy, yet that we are always to hold that event in view and to conduct ourselves accordingly, and that it becomes us to know and profit from the many and singular advantages we possess…If, notwithstanding every effort, the enemy should advance within reach of the capital, a great action must take place, but at such a distance as to allow the prospect of rallying and making a second stand in case of a repulse."

Action of Infantry:

"Nothing can be so strongly and frequently inculcated into our infantry of every description as the advantages they possess in attacking the enemy who has few or no cavalry to offend them, while on all occasions they enjoy the fullest support from our own, for active individuals and light infantry may remain in perfect safety within the smallest distance of such an enemy, watching every opportunity of distressing him, and larger bodies of infantry can never be pressed or overtaken if their rear is clear and their cavalry bold and active. By dint of repetition every soldier should be brought to understand that, even if he is worsted in action and compelled to fall back, his duty and honour require him to stop and rally as soon as possible; that he need never hurry, and that he is perfectly safe at a quarter mile distance from an enemy, who has no cavalry to make quick pursuit, therefore, that he ought to face about, form, and again advance or retire in a cool, soldier-like manner, and, in doing this, from his peculiar advantage, he is always protected by his own cavalry. But, above all, it must be impressed upon him that, although retiring and falling back gradually before the enemy may at first be ordered and necessary, to allow the force of the country to collect, yet our great object is to attack him on every favourable opportunity, and that not so much by fire, which is merely defensive, as by the bayonet and by that bold, manly and vigorous exertion which must inspire soldiers fighting for their religion, liberty and constitution. For, however successful the enemy may seem to be at first, and however long it may be necessary to postpone our general attack upon him, the moment will arrive when, by our accumulated numbers and united efforts, we shall overwhelm and may extirpate an army of unprincipled and merciless invaders."

After this rousing call to action the instruction continues with details of the disposition of the light infantry, cavalry and field artillery.

Appendix C
Burial of Sir John Moore, by Rev. Charles Wolfe (1791-1823).

Not a drum was heard, not a funeral note,
As his corse to the rampart we hurried;
Not a soldier discharged his farewell shot
O'er the grave where our hero was buried.

We buried him darkly at the dead of night,
The sods with our bayonets turning,
By the struggling moonbeam's misty light,
And the lantern dimly burning.

No useless coffin enclosed his breast,
Nor in sheet nor shroud we wound him;
But he lay like a warrior taking his rest,
With his martial cloak around him.

Few and short were the prayers we said,
And we spoke not a word of sorrow;
But we steadfastly gaz'd on the face that was dead;
And we bitterly thought of the morrow.

We thought, as we hollow'd his narrow bed,
And smooth'd down his lonely pillow,
That the foe and the stranger would tread o'er his head,
And we far away on the billow!

Lightly they'll talk of the spirit that's gone,
And o'er his cold ashes upbraid him;
But little he'll reck, if they let him sleep on
In the grave where a Briton has laid him.

But half of our heavy task was done
When the clock struck the hour for retiring:
And we heard the distant and random gun
Of the enemy, sullenly firing.

Slowly and sadly we laid him down,
From the field of his fame fresh and gory;
We carved not a line and we raised not a stone-
But we left him alone with his glory.

APPENDIX D
Full text of the letter written by Dedea Redanies

Letter to Mrs Back, mother of Caroline and Maria, translated from German into English.
Dearest Mother Back – On the first lines I pray to forgive the awful occurrence to the unlucky Dedea Redanies which I committed on my very dear Caroline and Maria Back yesterday morning; at five o'clock I perpetrated the horrible deed. Scarcely I am able to write by heart break for my ever memorable Caroline and Maria. The cause of this deed is – 1. I heard that Caroline is not in the family way as I first believed – 2. Because Caroline intends to go to Woolwich – 3. That I cannot stay with my very dear Caroline it made my heart so confused till at last the unhappy thought came into my head that Caroline rather may die from my hands, than to allow Caroline's love being bestowed upon another.

However I did not intend to murder also Maria her sister; but not having other opportunity and as she was in my way I could not do otherwise than stab her too.

Dear Mother Back – Saturday evening when I came I had not the least trace of this awful act. But as I learned that my dear Caroline gave me back my likeness and as she told me she would leave I did not know any other way in my heartbreak than to go to the Cutlers and I brought a poniard which divided the hearty lovers.

Arm in arm I brought both my dearest souls in the world over to the unlucky place near the road before Folkestone and requested them to sit down. But the grass being wet they refused to do so and I directed then Caroline to go forward and I went behind Maria into whose heart I run the dagger. With a dull cry she sank down. With a most broken heart I rushed then after Caroline, lifting the poniard in my hand towards her. Dear Dedea cried she with a half dead voice and fell down with weeping eyes. Then I rushed over her and gave her the last kisses as an everlasting remembrance.

I could live a more dreadful hour in my life than that was, and from my broken heart I knew not where my senses were, and I took as a lasting keepsake both the black shawls of Maria and my dear Caroline as a mourning suit for me leaving the awful spot with weeping eyes and a broken heart.

Never I shall forget my dear Caroline and Maria and the poniard remains covered with the blood of Maria and Caroline with me until it will pierce my own breast and I shall see my dear Maria and Caroline in the eternal life.

Farewell and be not troubled about the blissfully deceased angels of God and forgive the unhappy ever weeping

Dedea Redanies

3 August 1856

APPENDIX E

Lyrics of the Ballad, 'The Folkestone Murder'

Kind friends come pay attention and listen to my song
It is about a murder, it won't detain you long
'Twas near the town of Folkestone this shocking deed was done
Maria and sweet Caroline were murdered by Switzerland John.

He came unto their parents' house at nine o'clock one night
But little did poor Caroline think he owed her any spite.
"Will you walk with me, dear Caroline?" the murderer did say,
And she agreed to accompany him to Shorncliffe Camp next day.

Said the mother to the daughter "You'd better stay at home.
It is not fit for you to go with that young man alone.
You'd better take your sister to go along with you,
Then I have no objection, dear daughter, you may go."

Early next morning, before the break of day
Maria and sweet Caroline from Dover town did stray.
But before they reached to Folkestone the villain drew a knife,
Maria and sweet Caroline he took away their lives.

Down on the ground the sisters fell, all in their blooming years
For mercy cried, "We're innocent", their eyes were filled with tears.
He plunged the knife into their breasts, their lovely breasts so deep,
He robb'd them of their own sweet lives and left them there to sleep.

Three times he kissed their pale cold cheeks as they lay on the ground,
He took the capes from off their backs, for on him they were found.
He said "Farewell dear Caroline, your blood my hands have stained.
No more on earth shall I see you, but in heaven we'll meet again."

Early next morning their bodies they were found
At a lonely spot called Steady Hall, a-bleeding on the ground.
And if ever you go unto that spot, these letters you will find
Cut deeply in the grass so green: Maria and Caroline.

When the news it reached their parents' ears, they cried, "What shall we do?
Maria has been murdered, and lovely Caroline too"
They pulled and tore their old grey hair, in sorrow and in shame
And tears they rolled in torrents from their poor aged cheeks.

This murderer has been taken, his companions to him deny
And he is sent to Maidstone and is condemned to die
He said, "Farewell" to all his friends "In this world I am alone
And have to die for murder, far from my native home."

"The dismal bell is tolling, the scaffold I must prepare
I trust in heaven my soul shall rest and meet dear Caroline there.
Now all young man take warning from this sad fate of mine
To the memory of Maria Back and lovely Caroline".

Appendix F

A Short History of Small Arms, by Captain A.J. Parsons, printed in 1958

The history of small arms can be discussed under two and probably three headings. Firstly the musket, a smooth bored, heavy and inaccurate weapon in use from 1600 to the Crimean War. Secondly, the rifle, which first became a general issue in the 1850s. Finally, the self-loading rifle, the latest development.

Matchlock Harquebus :

The first musket to be used was the Matchlock Harquebus from 1600 to 1700. To load and fire it required some 30 separate drill motions and the time required to fire one shot was about a quarter of an hour.

The mechanism for this weapon was such that it was not possible to determine the actual firing time in relation to the pulling of the "tricker". It was necessary, therefore, to hold on aim for some considerable time, not knowing when the gun would go off. As a result the firer got rather bored and when subsequently it did go off he might not be on aim. It was therefore, amongst other things, very inaccurate.

Flintlock Musket:

The Matchlock Harquebus was superseded by the Flintlock Musket. This was a big improvement because it was now possible to guarantee roughly when it would go off, i.e., a second after powder had been lit. Thus there was an increase in accuracy.

The cumbersome firing procedure of the Harquebus was reduced considerably by a flint, which was fixed in the cock so that when the cock fell it struck against the steel of the hammer, opening the pan and making a shower of sparks. Some of these flew into the pan, igniting the priming powder and there was then a pause of about a second before the gun went off.

In the case of the musket the firer was given a bayonet for his protection, especially against cavalry.

Brown Bess :

By far the most famous of Flintlock Muskets was Brown Bess. This weapon was issued in 1700 and was still going strong in the Crimean War. As with all smooth bore weapons, the accuracy was still incredibly poor however.

During the Napoleonic Wars the government of the day issued some anti-invasion instructions and the people were told that "Any degree of precision with a common musket is not to be reckoned on at a greater distance than from 50 to 60 paces."

Training with Brown Bess was extremely rudimentary. The target for recruits was a round one eight feet in diameter, at a distance of 30 yards, then 50 yards and for trained soldiers, 100 yards. Shooting beyond this range was considered rather more from an interest point of view than for any military reason. Few could hit a house at 100 yards. With such inaccuracy, refinements of sighting were useless. There were, in fact, no sights at all except for a small knob near the muzzle which acted as a foresight to give the rough general direction. There was no backsight and it was difficult to judge elevation. The Platoon Commander had to see that the barrels were not too high and not too low or the bullets rolled out. There was no question of accuracy with this type of weapon.

Brown Bess was, however, a most remarkable weapon and lasted for 150 years. Originally a flintlock weapon, its firing mechanism was later modified. It was the weapon initially taught by the School of Musketry.

Brown Bess was used by Marlborough at the Battle of Blenheim in 1704, by Wellington at Waterloo in 1815 and was still going strong in the Crimean War.

The Rifle:

The principle of rifling whereby the bullet was kept on an even flight by spinning it by means of a rifled barrel was thought out long before it was actually applied in war.

To be effective the bullet had to grip the grooves of the barrel and difficulty was experienced in getting the bullet down the barrel from the muzzle end and a ramrod had to be used for this purpose. This meant difficult and slow loading and for many years the rifle had a slower rate of fire than the Musket. Because of this difficulty the rifle was only issued to the Green Jackets, who were specially raised (95th) and armed with it. Armed with the rifle, they were far more accurate than the rest of the army.

After the first shot, fouling was deposited by the black powder left in the barrel which completely filled the grooves and prevented the spin of the bullet, thus defeating the object of rifling. This difficulty was not finally overcome until 1800 with the discovery of cordite.

The first rifle to be issued to the experimental Rifle Corps of picked sharpshooters, which ultimately became the Rifle Brigade, was the Baker Rifle, named after a gunsmith in Whitechapel.

The issue of this new rifle caused the Green Jackets to develop their own form of drill which has persisted till today. The firing positions were standing, kneeling, lying with barrel resting on the tall plumed hat, especially designed for the purpose, or lying on the back with rifle rested on the toes, and the sling round the feet to take the shock of discharge. The butt was on the breast.

Its advantages were its increased accuracy, range, ease of training and weight, but the firing speed was comparatively slow.

In 1838 the Rifle Brigade were equipped with the Brunswick Rifle, but it was not until 1851 that the rifle became a general issue.

The French took the lead between 1830 and 1850. They devised a means of getting the bullet into the barrel from the muzzle end, just small enough to go in and expand at the moment of firing. As a result of the French lead the first British rifle for general issue was the Minie.

One of the advantages of the Minie over previous weapons was its sighting, with 1,000 yards maximum and 100 yards minimum. The bullet could be dropped into the barrel more easily, there was an increased range and an increase in the rate of fire, but it was one pound heavier. The general issue was not completed until after the Crimean War and it took ten years to equip the Army. We still had no magazine, no really accurate sighting and no bolt action, and still could not load from the breech. The Minie was, however, a tremendous step forward and The Times correspondent in the Crimea wrote the following:

"It is the King of weapons, Inkerman proved it. The Regiments of the 4th Division and the Marines, armed with the old and much belauded Brown Bess, could do nothing with their thin line of fire against the massive multitudes of the Muscovite Infantry, but the volleys of the Minie cleft them like the hand of the destroying Angel and they fell like autumn leaves before them."

In 1854 the Minie was succeeded by the Enfield which was again another definite step forward. There was a reduction in calibre and sighting was more accurate. In fact, field artillery still with smooth bore barrels, were temporarily outdistanced by the rifle. It took the Army a long time to adjust itself to the new improvements afforded by the rifle. So strong was the influence of Brown Bess that even as late as 1885, Volunteers, the modern TA, got their efficiency grant if they did a set number of drills and fired 60 rounds in the direction of the target.

In 1866 the Enfield was still loaded from the muzzle end. One of the greatest difficulties was to find a safe way of loading from the breech. Every time it was tried, someone was injured as the flaming gases leaked out violently backwards between the joints of the breech. It was reported in The Illustrated London News of 24th February, 1855 that a trial had been carried out at Hythe of a newly invented self-breech-loading and priming carbine. Sixty shots had been fired with it in seven minutes and out of that number, at a range of 100 yards, 47 struck the bull's-eye.

This problem had, however, been overcome by the Prussians who, largely as a result, in 1848 overran Denmark in three weeks and, some years later, Austria in six weeks. It was not until 1867 that we realised how enormously the speed of fire was increased by breech action and so in that year the Enfield was modified for breech-loading by what was known as the Snider action—an American design.

In 1871 the Army adopted the Martini Henry rifle and later in 1888 the Lee Metford rifle and for the first time we see the introduction of the magazine.

APPENDIX G

Extract from The Illustrated London News, 16th July 1859

Travellers who, urged by duty or pleasure find themselves speeding along that European highway which leads to London from Paris, via Dover, can hardly fail to notice a strange looking assemblage of dwelling-houses situated a few hundred yards south of the line, some three miles on the London side of the hilly town of Folkestone. A first glance conveys to the mind merely an idea of a moderate-sized town; but a few intermittent glimpses... develop strange and puzzling peculiarities. There are no commanding edifices visible; no parish church, with its steeple crowned tower; no market place; no suburban mansions or villas. The houses are mathematically disposed in rectangular parallelograms, and are, moreover, all exactly alike in size, shape and colour. Can it be that this part of England is subject to earthquakes? For, observe, those houses are mostly of wood and have only one floor. The colouring, too-how strange! Every house is painted a sort of Venetian red, with white windows and doors, and black roof. If you are travelling for pleasure, take advice; stop at Folkestone and explore this ligneous town. The journey is by no means irksome, and if it were you would find plenty to reward you for your exertions.

You take a fly at the station and, having given the necessary instructions to the driver, away you rattle up and down the streets of Folkestone, and you are soon in a position to substantiate the assertion made by the author of the "Ingoldsby Legends" that this town is not built on seven hills, but seventy. Having achieved the passage of these Alpine streets, you find yourself rolling smoothly on a well made road, on one side of which is the sea, and on the other, fine bold and picturesque cliffs. Driving two miles along the road, you are in the village of Sandgate, which consists of one street, built between the foot of the cliffs and the beach. You leave your trap at one of the two weather-board hotels, and a few minutes' walk up somewhat steep and ragged paths brings you to the plateau known as Shorncliffe, whereon stands the wooden town – Shorncliffe Camp, accurately depicted in The Illustrated London News on the occasion of the Prince of Wales presenting colours to the 100th Regiment there a few months ago. Situated as it is, it is but little known to the public, nor is it emblazoned on the roll of fame like Aldershot.

One glance round the elevated plain on which you stand, and you see at once that it is one of the finest sites in the country for a large camp, whether for purpose of instruction or of offensive or defensive operations. Its commanding situation; its position with regard to the Continent, from which it is distant 15 miles; its proximity to the sea; the fine, pure, healthy air; the shelter it receives from the second range of cliffs about two miles to the north; the size of the plain, which is large enough to encamp the whole British Army; and its capability of being easily fortified, all point it out as the most eligible spot in England for the chief camp.

At present Shorncliffe accommodates only 3000 men – namely, three regiments of the Line, four field batteries of artillery, a battalion of the Military Train, a squadron of Cavalry and a company of engineers.

The huts are arranged on three sides of a parallelogram, the eastern end being open. Near the centre of this opening stand the guard-room, the flagstaff, and a cannon which is fired every day at or about noon, and gives the military time, for it is neither local nor Greenwich; and, judging by it, the sun must keep his meridian appointments but with indifferent punctuality.

We will now look and see how complete most of the arrangements are. As we came up the hill we passed a steam engine. Beneath the house that contains the engine are large tanks, onto which water is conveyed from a reservoir three miles away. The engine then forces the water into a cistern placed on a lofty tower situated on the plateau, and pipes from this cistern carry water to every part of the camp. The cook houses are all fitted with Captain Grant's apparatus which, with a small consumption of fuel enable the men to perform all of the culinary operations… In addition to the usual ablution houses, there are 40 baths fitted with every regard to comfort and decency. It is hoped that similar sanitary conveniences are placed in inland barracks; here they are hardly essentially necessary, seeing that a man may stand at the door of his hut and almost throw stones into the sea.

The Provost is a less pleasing feature. It resembles other military prisons as much as wooden huts can resemble stone buildings. Those large iron huts are barrack stores and are fitted with such articles of furniture as barrack rooms are supplied with. There is a solitary brick building, without windows, surrounded by a high wall and surmounted by a lightning conductor; that is the powder magazine, unpleasantly near the huts; but the fact is, it existed before the camp was erected, and it is supposed that the Government could not afford to move so costly a building to a place where an accidental explosion would be less likely to prove fatal.

The church is built after the same style as the huts, only upon a much more extensive scale. It is fitted so that during the week it may serve as a school. The churchyard is picturesquely situated on the spur of a hill which runs out into the romantic-looking valley of Seabrook. Here traces may be seen of the Foreign Legion, for which this camp was originally erected, in the wooden and stone crosses placed at the head of some of the graves. Although the huts have been erected for more than four years, they are in excellent condition, as weatherproof as wooden buildings can be. The roofs are covered with felt and tar, and the walls externally with Torbay iron paint, which renders the wood imperishable.

To the north-east of the camp stands a small brick barrack adapted for one field battery of artillery. This was erected and occupied long before the camp. At the diagonally opposite corner (the south-east) is a half-finished redoubt. This was thrown up for practice by the troops, encamped here under the command of Sir John Moore, in 1808, just prior to that general's embarkation for Spain, where, within four months of his landing, he received his death wound.

The distance from Shorncliffe to the School of Musketry at Hythe is between two and three miles. The men in camp are consequently marched there in detachments for practice, which is decidedly a very advantageous arrangement.

Appendix H

The British Volunteer System, by The Rt. Hon. Earl Brownlow, formerly Under-Secretary of State for War.

The early years of the century found England in the possession of a large body of volunteers. They were not a part of the permanent military organization of the country, but were raised in a hurry, and for a special purpose, and were only intended to meet a sudden emergency. At that period, Napoleon I had massed a great army at Boulogne in sight of the British coast; but the British cruisers held the Channel, and day after day and month after month passed, until the naval battle of Trafalgar put an end forever to his ambitious dream of the conquest of England. It was to meet this contingency that the Volunteers of 1803 were raised, and the danger having been averted, they were disbanded and never brought together again.

With the organization and efficiency of this force, this article is in no way concerned, and it is only mentioned here to explain that volunteering for defence of the country is no new idea, but that the volunteers of 1803 have no relation to those of 1858. They served their purpose; they came together to the number of 463,000 men, and when the emergency ceased, they died out and disappeared.

They seem to have incurred at that time a certain amount of "chaff" on account of their somewhat crude idea of military duties, and it is said that one regiment having repeatedly pointed out to Mr. Pitt that they only volunteered to repel invasion, and were on no account to be sent out of the country, he replied that he would promise not to send them away "except in the case of invasion."

There is, however, one volunteer corps – the Honourable Artillery Company of the City of London – which is quite exceptional. It dates from the time of Henry VII, at which period it wore a picturesque dress, had nothing to do, and "did it very well;" and it consists of artillery, cavalry and infantry. It is not a "company" in the military sense, but has many of the attributes of the City of London companies, and has property and funds of its own.

This ancient corps has its counterpart in the Honourable Artillery Company of Boston in the United States, the members of which some time ago visited London and received a cordial welcome as a link between the Old and the New Worlds.

Until 1858, the Honourable Artillery Company was the only old-established Volunteer Corps. At that time, the country was thirsting for peace and rest. The Crimean War had disclosed a state of military disorganization in the army which had caused misery and disaster to the troops during the war, and it was felt that only the bravery and pluck of the officers and men had saved the country from actual defeat; but when peace with Russia had been obtained, no time was given for reorganisation. The Indian mutiny, following on the heels of the Crimean war, called forth all the resources of the Empire; but, when tranquillity was again restored, the public mind once more turned to the contemplation of army reform.

The opportunity seemed favourable. The Emperor of the French was in close alliance with England, and we were at peace with all European nations. There was no cloud upon the political horizon, and there seemed every prospect that this happy condition of things would be lasting.

At that moment, a bolt from the blue – as far-reaching as it was unexpected – spread dismay throughout Europe. On January 14th, 1858, an Italian named Felice Orsini, attempted the life of the Emperor Napoleon III by throwing a bomb under the carriage containing the Emperor and Empress as it was drawing up at the door of the opera house; and although the intended victims escaped unhurt, the missile spread destruction all round the spot where the outrage was committed.

It soon became known that the would-be assassin had hatched his conspiracy and manufactured his bombs in England; and, in the excitement that ran like wildfire through the French army, a hundred French colonels signed a petition to the Emperor, praying him to put himself at their head and lead them against "Perfidious Albion." It was not certain whether the Emperor would be able to resist the pressure thus put upon him, and the ugly fact of a possible invasion of our coasts stared us in the face. It was felt that our army – most of which was abroad – was inadequate to cope with the large forces which were at the disposal of France, if they should once gain a footing on our shores, and excitement little short of panic ensued.

The people of England demanded arms that they might at least make a stubborn resistance, and the volunteer force of Great Britain sprang into life.

In its infancy its constitution was hardly worthy to be called "organisation." A large number of enthusiastic civilians of all classes enrolled themselves under officers who, for the most part, had little or no military training, and drilled and equipped themselves in isolated companies. All worked with an energy which only determination, coupled with a grave sense of danger, could inspire. Drill went on in every town in England and Scotland; rifle butts were hastily erected, and the first rudiments of shooting were taught by sergeant-instructors from the regular army. But in spite of all this activity the volunteer army was a mere "crowd of men with muskets," without transport, without battalion formation, and with only one suit of clothes apiece; and with such a force the only rôle assigned to them was to rush to meet the enemy, to line the hedges and walls in inclosed country; to worry and annoy the invaders in every possible way, and to die fighting to the last in order that the regular army and the militia might gain time to assemble and make their dispositions for defence, The action of the French franc-tireurs in the Franco-Prussian War shows how much may be done by such means. While matters were in this state, the scare which had created the volunteer force came to an end as suddenly as it had arisen. Napoleon III, loyal to his alliance with England, succeeded in quieting his excitable colonels, and the danger of immediate invasion was averted.

The volunteers now entered upon the most critical period of their whole history. The officers of the regular army looked upon them as almost useless, and either gave them good-natured but half-hearted support, or advocated their being disbanded altogether; for the British officers of that day believed only in long-service troops, drilled with all the precision of machines; controlled when in barracks with an iron discipline, and perfect in parade movements. The country would not hear of conscription; the army would not hear of short service. So for years nothing was done to reorganize the army, and the volunteers were left to live and die in an atmosphere of neglect or ridicule.

A slight advance was made by the scattered companies being formed into provisional battalions for purpose of drill, and being given a retired officer or militia officer as adjutant; and as they marched through the streets headed by the band, a crowd of street urchins ran beside them shouting such ribald cries as "Who shot the dog?" "How are yer poor feet?" and (to the mounted officers), "How much an hour for yer horse, gov'nor?" And when the battalion had reached its drill ground and deployed into line, the gamins formed line opposite to them, waiting, like the French line at Fontenoy, for the English to fire first. Then, as the rattle of the locks proclaimed the volley which terminated the "platoon" exercise, they fell down with shrieks and groans, and writhed in simulated agony of death on the battlefield, while the lookers on shouted with laughter at the performance.

When the parade was dismissed each individual volunteer went home in a storm of chaff, and the clever pencil of John Leech made fun of them in "Punch." How they survived this ordeal seems now a miracle; but survive it they did, and set to work with a will to increase their efficiency.

It is obvious that an armed man – whether regular soldier or volunteer – is of little value for fighting purposes, unless he can shoot fairly well with a rifle; and the volunteers, recognizing this fact, proceeded at once to establish a shooting organisation throughout the country. The centre and head of this organization was, and is, the National Rifle Association, which held its meetings at Wimbledon until they were transferred to Bisley.

In every county or district, an association was formed under "Wimbledon Rules," which held its meetings once a year, and battalion and company meetings also offered a chance of winning prizes to those who were not sufficiently expert in the use of the rifle to compete at Wimbledon. Thus an inducement was given to every volunteer to practice rifle shooting, in addition to the class firing ordered by the volunteer regulations.

The artillery have an association of their own called the National Artillery Association, which is quite separate from the National Rifle Association, and holds its meetings at Shoeburyness. It works on strictly military lines, and forms a camp where the mounting and dismounting of heavy guns, etc., as well as target practice, is a part of the regular training.

This, briefly, is the organization which, with some alterations and improvements, has continued to the present day.

The first meeting at Wimbledon opened on July 2, 1860, when Queen Victoria fired the first shot, with a rifle fixed in a rest and laid by the most experienced rifle-shot of the day, and the "bull's-eye" flag went up amidst the cheers of a large crowd of spectators. To promote shooting at moving objects, a life-sized stag made of iron was mounted on a small railway, and ran down an incline on one side of the range, and nearly to the top of the incline on the other side, on the principle of a switchback railway, the shot having to be fired between two white posts, thirty yards apart. Sir Edwin Landseer, the celebrated animal painter, drew the stag life-size, and this splendid sketch and the "Queen's" target are preserved by the National Rifle Association as their two most valued treasures.

In the year 1883 a team of the American National Guard came over to England to shoot against an English volunteer team. At the beginning of the match, the visitors gained a considerable lead; but at the long ranges the English team not only wiped out their loss, but succeeded in securing a hard-fought victory. In the evening both teams dined with the president of the National Rifle Association, on which occasion there were present Her Royal Highness the Duchess of Teck, the Duke of Teck, and the Hon. J. R. Lowell, the Minister of the United States in England. After dinner the rule of the association that no speeches are to be made was so far relaxed as to allow of the health of the American team being proposed by the president; and

Mr. Lowell, in returning thanks for his countrymen, made one of those short and happy speeches which did so much to promote a cordial feeling between the two nations. He said on this occasion: "May God grant that in all rifle competitions between the two nations, all the rifles may always be pointed the same way" - a sentiment cordially echoed at the present day on both sides of the Atlantic.

Englishmen noted with interest during the late war of the United States with Spain, the readiness with which volunteers came forward in large numbers and at very short notice to serve their country. English volunteers in particular observed with admiration their cheerful endurance of thirst, hunger and privations of all sorts, in occasional circumstances of peculiar hardship.

That they should show courage in the field was taken for granted; but that with such short training, and in spite of hasty and, in certain cases, inadequate equipment, these citizen soldiers should develop such splendid qualities of discipline, self-restraint and self-reliance was the subject of much and hearty praise among English military critics.

The system pursued by the National Rifle Association has worked well, and although it is described as "pot-hunting" by those who wish to decry it, it has produced many first-rate shots, and may fairly claim to have carried out the object for which it was formed.

It would be impossible in the limited space of a magazine article, and would be tedious to the general reader, to treat in detail of the improvements in organization which have been carried out, from time to time, in the volunteer force; but a few words on the present state of the force may not be out of place.

The battalions are now united into brigades, commanded by brigadiers who have most of them served in the regular army, assisted by brigade majors, who are all retired officers, and a sufficient staff. These brigades assemble yearly in camp, and when at Aldershot or any other military centre come under military law, and take part in field days with the regular troops. The men learn all the duties of camp life; to pitch and strike tents, to cook and to make themselves at home in camp. A hearty and cheerful spirit animates all ranks, and the men look upon the annual training in camp in the light of a holiday, and are cheerfully prepared to perform readily all the various duties in return for the change of scene and work, and amusement and relaxation after the parades are over for the day.

As to their fighting qualities, it can only be said that they have never been tested, but there is no reason to believe that they would fight with less pluck and determination than any other men of the Anglo-Saxon race. In case of emergency, they would fight in their own country for all they hold most dear, and history has proved over and over again that men fighting under these circumstances are not to be despised, even by the best-disciplined and most highly trained troops. As regards "discipline," that word which may mean so much or so little, it must be remembered that the average volunteer lives a disciplined life. He is not a raw boy taken from the ploughshare, nor is he a young man of fast habits who has got into some minor scrape; but he is a respectable tradesman or superior mechanic, who has a character to lose, and I have myself seen a man, when brought up for judgment in camp, tremble and turn pale at the thought of being dismissed from the service, or sent out of camp in disgrace, which, when not camped with regular troops, is the only punishment the commanding officer has power to inflict.

Such a man returns to his native town or village with a mark against him. He gets "chaffed" by the men, and - what is more important - is despised by the women. It is known that he has failed to acquit himself with credit in a duty which he has voluntarily undertaken to perform, and he has to bear the consequences.

From want of experience a volunteer sentry will, from time to time, present arms to a showy uniform, and a smart non-commissioned officer of cavalry in full uniform will receive greater honour than a general in a blue coat; but this comes from want of knowledge of details, and not from want of discipline.

A simple and practical form of drill has been introduced, which is far better suited to the volunteers than the slow, antiquated drill of thirty years ago. It is easily and rapidly acquired, and thus time is available for the teaching of outpost duty, advance and rear guards, and many other details of which in their infancy the volunteers were profoundly ignorant. The officers of the new school now at the head of the army, who no longer cling to old traditions because they were good enough in their youth, recognize that modern weapons have altered the conditions of warfare, and have long ago discarded the drill of the time of the Duke of Wellington, who for many years opposed the introduction of the percussion musket because he said "the men would fire away their ammunition too quickly." The volunteers are now recognized as an integral part of the defences of the country, and in consequence panic from fear of invasion is now unknown. The necessity for conscription, which is hateful to the country, and now only exists in a very mild and modified form in the militia ballot act, which is never carried out, has been averted, and it is therefore fair to claim that the volunteers carry out in an adequate measure the purpose for which they were raised, and England sleeps the sounder for the knowledge that the manhood of the population is armed for her defence.

There is, however, another important advantage which has been gained for the country. In old days the average villager had no idea of the duties of a soldier, whose occupation was described as "being shot at for a shilling a day," and a story is told of a mother parting from her son, who had enlisted, saying to the recruiting sergeant: "How many hours a day will the poor lad have to fight, Mr. Soldier?" The idea existed that the soldier's time was divided between fighting and debauchery, and the enlistment of a son was looked upon as a family disgrace. Many villagers never saw troops under arms in their whole lives, and the soldier and civilian were as much separated as if they were different races. This feeling is growing less and less yearly, and there is every hope that it will die out in the near future. This improvement is partly owing to amelioration in the condition of the soldiers, and the care shown for their welfare by the authorities in modern days; but it is also due to the fact that civilians are now able to give some attention to, and gain practical knowledge of, military affairs by means of volunteering. They wear a uniform, and are proud of it; they come into contact with regular troops in military centres, and make friends with the men and learn from them the details of military life. Tommy Atkins is delighted to make friends with the volunteer, and the volunteer takes a military pride in "chumming" with Tommy Atkins, and thus they gain a mutual respect and regard for each other. The days are long passed when the volunteers were alternately inflated by exaggerated praise or depressed by scorn and ridicule. They have taken their place as auxiliary to the regular army, anxious only to prepare themselves for the duties which would be assigned to them in case of emergency, and desiring to act up to their motto of "Defence, not defiance."

APPENDIX I

A Soldier's Tale

Many of the young men of Canada who volunteered to fight in the Great War were, in fact, British. During the late nineteenth and early twentieth centuries, they had flocked to Canada to seek their fortunes in that rugged country, where opportunity and adventure beckoned. Among them was Clarence Dove Booth.

The Great Outdoors. The life that Clarrie Booth gave up when he joined the Canadian Army in 1915.

Clarence, who was universally known as Clarrie, was born in 1892 and grew up in Hythe where his father was the Steward of the Oddfellows Club. As a young man Clarrie learned to play the piano, but it was as a footballer that he was best known, playing for Hythe Town football club. In 1912, the twenty year-old announced that he was going to follow his older sister, Daisy, to Canada and the local newspaper reported the loss of a fine player from the town's team. Daisy had married Fred Ames, an engineer, and gone with him when he found work on the construction of the Canadian Pacific Railroad. Fred could probably have helped his brother-in-law to find work on the railway but, apart from playing the piano, Clarrie's skills were in his feet not his hands. Instead, he found work as a storekeeper near Edmonton, Alberta, but he took every opportunity to explore and photograph the surrounding landscape which was so different to the rolling hills of his native North Downs.

When war broke out in 1914, men flocked to the recruiting stations across Canada. Clarrie, probably deterred by the talk that 'it would be over by Christmas', watched and waited. As news arrived of the heavy losses in the first few months of the war, this optimism gave way to the reality of a long and bitter struggle ahead. Clarrie waited no longer and decided to volunteer for the Canadian army, walking into the recruiting office in Edmonton on the 15th January 1915. At 5 feet 6 inches and a physique described as 'fair' by the medical officer, he was passed as fit for active service and was taken on strength by the 51st Overseas Battalion, Canadian Expeditionary Force; his regimental number was 436419.

All Aboard. Having signed up, the recruits boarded the train in Edmonton for the journey to their initial training camp in Calgary.

Within days, the new recruit was packed off to Sarcee Camp at Calgary for his basic training. The camp was named after the Native American Indian tribe that had roamed the land a generation before. Nine months later, on the 11th September 1915, the 51st Battalion embarked aboard the S.S. Metagama at Montreal and set sail for England, eventually arriving at Shorncliffe Camp in Folkestone on the 30th September. Private Booth was assigned to the 49th (Edmonton) Battalion Canadian Infantry, part of the Canadian 3rd Division. Clarrie was back home and proudly visited friends and family in his new khaki uniform with the brightly polished maple leaf badge on his cap.

Unlike the 2nd Division before them, the 3rd Division were given no time to undertake additional training whilst at Shorncliffe. The war of attrition on the Western Front demanded that more and more men be thrown into the trenches, many of them ill-prepared for the horrors that confronted them. The 49th Battalion marched from Shorncliffe to Folkestone Harbour on the 9th October and boarded the troopships for

Sarcee Camp, Canada. This is where Clarrie did his basic training.

Boulogne. No sooner had Private Booth landed in France than he was given a pick, something against which anyone who knew Clarrie would have urged caution. The predictable result was that he sustained an injured hand and had to report to the Field Ambulance for treatment. After a swift recovery he was able to rejoin his unit. The 3rd Division saw little action over the next few months but, in the spring 1916, the three Canadian Divisions were sent forward to relieve the British troops to the east of Ypres. The British had battled for nearly two years to keep the high ground of Mount Sorrel and Tor Top (also known as Hill 62), but as spring moved into summer, the sector seemed quiet. These positions just to the east of Armagh and Sanctuary Woods and with a clear view to Ypres a few miles to the west were of key strategic importance. Unknown to the Allies, the German High Command had spent six weeks preparing an attack on the two summits; mines had been laid and additional artillery had been brought forward. At dawn on the 2nd June, after a devastating artillery barrage, the German XIII (Wuttemburg) Corps attacked. The Canadians suffered heavy casualties but despite desperately fighting to retain their ground, they were forced to concede Mount Sorrel and Tor Top. The Canadians had not yet achieved the reputations that they would earn on the Somme or Vimy Ridge and they were devastated at the loss of these key positions. Reserves were brought forward and a counterattack was planned for the next day, the 3rd June. The 7th Canadian Brigade was called forward, and this included Private Booth in the 49th Battalion. The signal to attack was due to be given at 6.00am but confusion arose when six signal rockets were prematurely ignited. What should have been three simultaneous attacks became piecemeal and the Germans were able to concentrate their fire on each front in turn. Although the Canadians were able to close some gaps in the line, by early afternoon they had to fall back to their start positions. During the fierce fighting, some of it hand to hand, Private Booth was shot; a bullet or shrapnel caught his right shoulder, smashing his collar bone. He managed to return to his lines and was evacuated to the No 1 Canadian Military Hospital at Etaples. From here, on the 30th June, Booth was transferred to the Royal Herbert Hospital at Woolwich. Meanwhile, the depleted Canadian battalions continued to fight for the return of Mount Sorrel culminating in an assault by two composite battalions on the 13th June. Under cover of a smoke screen the men moved forward and succeeded in dislodging the Germans. Over the past two weeks the Canadians had lost 8430 officers and men, killed, missing or wounded, but they had regained their pride and acquired a reputation for tenacity and hard fighting.

Wounded. Having been wounded at Ypres in June 1916, Clarrie was initially evacuated back to Shorncliffe.

Back in England, after treatment to his shoulder, Clarrie was sent to the Woodcote Park Convalescent Hospital in Epsom followed by two weeks home leave in Cheriton where the Booth family now lived at the Oddfellows Club in Broomfield Road. Where and when they had met is not known but the dashing young soldier had caught the eye of a 25 year-old young lady from Oxfordshire. Lilias May White was living on the King's Road in Chelsea in 1916 when she met Clarrie and they fell in love. A quiet wedding at Christ Church in Chelsea was followed by a honeymoon in Ramsgate, but then came separation as the soldier returned to Barracks and Lilias to London. The next few months must have been frustrating for Clarence as he was moved from one Canadian Convalescent Depot to another. He clearly could not return to active service with his shoulder wound, but

The Footballer. Unable to return to active duty, Clarrie was picked to play for the 21st. They went on to take the Championship in 1918. Clarrie is back row, far right.

what could he do? In June 1917, Clarrie arrived at Bramshott Camp near Aldershot and was posted to the 21st Reserve Battalion and it was here that his footballing skills were noticed; he was picked to play for the battalion team and travelled the country playing matches. The Canadian troops were keen sportsmen; in one year the YMCA supplied 132 footballs and the same number of baseball bats to the men. The competitions were good for morale and a large turnout was always assured. For Clarrie and his team there were successes; they took the Northern Command title, beating the 1st Battalion Machine Gun Corps by 6 goals to 2 at the Elland Road ground of Leeds United. In 1918, came the supreme prize when the 21st Reserve Battalion won the title of champions of the Canadian Military Forces (British Isles). The final was played at Seaford against the 11th Reserve Battalion, based at Shorncliffe. The Bramshott team took a three goal lead in the first half from which, despite a fight back in the second, the Shorncliffe men were unable to recover. Clarrie and his team mates were each presented with a gold winner's medal and the silver Championship trophy.

When not entertaining his comrades on the football field, Clarrie was part of a troupe of soldiers known as the Canadian Follies. Providing musical and comic entertainment, the men toured the Canadian camps helping to maintain the morale of the troops.

With the Armistice in November 1918 the process of demobilisation began, but it would be some months before Private Booth returned to civilian life. Postings to Ripon and Whitley kept him and Lilias apart, but at least he was given home leave over that Christmas to spend with his wife and their daughter, Edna, who had been born in February 1917. Unlike many of his fellow Canadians, even those who had married whilst in Britain, Clarrie did not return to Canada. Instead, when he was discharged from the army on the 6th June 1919, he and Lilias lived for a year in Wandsworth before moving to Folkestone and setting up home in Chart Road. According to his medical discharge papers, Clarrie had grown 3 inches in height since he had walked into the recruiting office in Alberta four years earlier and the physique which had only been described as 'fair' then was now 'robust'.

Clarrie and Lilias lived their lives happily in Folkestone, with two more children,

Clarence (always known as Eric) and Dennis. Clarrie continued to play football and also acquired a local reputation as a whist player. During World War II he joined the Post Office Home Guard detachment. Lilias died in 1969, with Clarence following in 1973, never having returned to Canada.

Clarrie, Lilias and baby Edna. This photo was taken in early 1919. Although the war was over, Clarrie had to wait until June for his demob.

Appendix J

List of fatalities caused by the Great Air Raid, 25th May 1917

SURNAME	FIRST NAMES	AGE	RESIDENCE	PLACE OF DEATH	DATE OF DEATH	NOTES
Arnold	May Alexandra	21	19 Bouverie Road East	injured Bouverie Road East, died Moore Barracks Hospital	25th May 1917	widow of a soldier, Bombardier F Arnold, CFA
Banks	Harold Hayward	25	20 Victoria Grove	injured in Bouverie Road East, died Westcliffe Military Hospital	26th May 1917	chauffeur
Barker	Mrs Eliza Mary	33	29 Bradstone Road	injured Tontine Street, died Royal Victoria Hospital	25th May 1917	
Bartleet	Maggie Grey	24 or 34	27 Connaught Road	Jointon Road	25th May 1917	wife of Sgt. Major Joseph J Bartleet RAMC
Beer	Annie	28	90 Blackbull Road	Tontine Street	25th May 1917	wife of Ernest Beer, marine fireman
Beer	Annie	2	90 Blackbull Road	Tontine Street	25th May 1917	daughter of Annie and Ernest Beer
Beer	Arthur Stephen	11	67 Bridge Street	Tontine Street	25th May 1917	son of Harry Beer, coal porter
Beer	William James	9	67 Bridge Street	Tontine Street	25th May 1917	son of Harry Beer, marine fireman
Bloodworth	George Henry	26		injured 21 Bouverie Road East, died Westcliffe Military Hospital	25th May 1917	private soldier
Bowbrick	Gertrude Elizabeth	12	81 Ashley Avenue	Tontine Street	25th May 1917	daughter of Mr Walter Bowbrick, builder's foreman
Bowbrick	Lily Caroline (Nellie)	55	81 Ashley Avenue	injured Tontine Street, died Royal Victoria Hospital	24th March 1925	wife of Mr Walter Bowbrick, builder's foreman.
				She remained in the hospital from 1917 until her death in 1925, paralysed from the waist down.		
Bowbrick	Mabel Esther	9	81 Ashley Avenue	Tontine Street	25th May 1917	daughter of Mr Walter Bowbrick, builder's foreman
Brockway	Sidney	63	17 Peter Street	Tontine Street	25th May 1917	Corporation outdoor employee
Burgin	Dorothy Lillian	16	21 Oak Road, Cheriton	Royal Victoria Hospital	31st May 1917	laundry worker, daughter of Mrs Mary Ann Ellender
Burke	David John	42	29 St Winifred Road	21 Bouverie Road East	25th May 1917	a boot and shoe repairer.
Burvill	Hilda Elizabeth	20	The Cottage, Blackbull Road	injured Tontine Street, died Royal Victoria Hospital	26th May 1917	daughter of Mr Albert Burvill, estate labourer
Butcher	George Edward	44	27 Alexandra Street	injured near Castle Inn, Foord, died Royal Victoria Hospital	6th Jun 1917	a coal carter
Cason	Annie Elizabeth	46	24 Military Avenue	Tontine Street	25th May 1917	wife of Arthur C Cason, barrack warden
Castle	Albert Edward	41	27 Wear Bay Crescent	Grange School, Shorncliffe Road	25th May 1917	naval pensioner and gardener
Chapman	Kathleen	16	Bates Hotel	injured 21 Bouverie Road East, died Royal Victoria Hospital	25th May 1917	housemaid at Bates Hotel, daughter of Alfred Chapman of Chilham Lees
Clark	William	12	24 Mead Road	injured Tontine Street, died at Westcliffe Military Hospital		boy scout, son of Stephen Clark

Surname	First name	Age	Address	Place	Date	Notes
Considine	Francis Henry	5	27 Oaks Road			son of a Canadian soldier
Cooper	Phyllis Amies	10	3 Warwick Terrace	injured Tontine Street, died Royal Victoria Hospital	26th May 1917	daughter of Mr Albert Wallace Cooper, butcher's assistant
Daniels	Albert Dennis	12	Coombe Farm Hawkinge	Tontine Street	25th May 1917	son of Mr Albert Daniels, farmer
Day	Frederick	52	4 Linden Crescent	Tontine Street	25th May 1917	grocer's assistant
Dicker	Edith Agnes	13	13 Richmond Street	Tontine Street	25th May 1917	daughter of Sarah and George Wilkie Dicker
Dicker	Sarah Jane	41	13 Richmond Street	Tontine Street	25th May 1917	wife of Mr George Wilkie Dicker, manager of the Maypole Dairy Co.
Down	Alfred Durrett	54	52 Royal Military Avenue			painter
Dukes	Florence Edith	18	3 Devonshire Place, Horn Street	Tontine Street	25th May 1917	daughter of Mr Henry Barfert Dukes, mercantile clerk, a housemaid home for her holiday
Dukes	Florence Elizabeth	51	3 Devonshire Place, Horn Street	Tontine Street	25th May 1917	wife of Mr Henry Barfert Dukes, mercantile clerk
Eales	Edith May	18	27 Dudley Road	injured Tontine Street, died Royal Victoria Hospital	26th May 1917	daughter of Mr Arthur Eales, marine porter, bookkeeper at Stokes Brothers. Died one day before her 18th birthday
Feist	Nellie	50	Coombe Farm, Hawkinge	Tontine Street	25th May 1917	married woman
Feist	Stanley Albert	5	Coombe Farm, Hawkinge	Tontine Street	25th May 1917	son of Mrs Nellie Feist
Francis	Florence	33	46 Foord Road	Tontine Street	25th May 1917	
Gould	Edward or Ernest Stephen	40	not known	injured Tontine Street, died Royal Victoria Hospital	25th May 1917	coal carter in the employ of Anderson and Co.
Graves	Richard Ashby	40		injured Tontine Street, died Royal Victoria Hospital	25th May 1917	stable man, Pavilion Shades Stables
Grimes	Edith Mary	24	14 Tontine Street	Tontine Street	25th May 1917	typist
Hall	William Henry		68 Tontine Street	injured Tontine Street, died Royal Victoria Hospital	27th May 1917	pork butcher
Hambley	Johannah Mary	67	32 Radnor Park Road	Tontine Street	25th May 1917	widow of Capt. Edgar Hambley, R.N.
Hambrook	Ethel	12	1 Invicta Road	Tontine Street		daughter of Mrs Hambrook
Harris	Caroline	35	144 High Street Cheriton	Tontine Street	25th May 1917	wife of Joseph or James Harris, Cyclist Corps
Harrison	Fanny or Annie	39	15 Bournemouth Road	Tontine Street	25th May 1917	spinster, no occupation
Hayes	Dennis William	2yrs 9 months	25 East Street			son of Martha Hayes, his father having been killed a year ago
Hayes	Martha Godden	30	25 East Street	Tontine Street	25th May 1917	widow of a soldier
Hayward	Louisa Alice	37	38 Thanet Gardens	Tontine Street	25th May 1917	wife of Pte. W Hayward, The Buffs
Hickman	Arthur David	5	93 Military Avenue	Tontine Street	25th May 1917	son of Sgt-Major Hickman, Royal Scots
Holloway	Mary Philhemina	9	13 Burrow Road	Tontine Street	25th May 1917	daughter of Mr Frederick Sidney Holloway, merchants clerk
Holloway	Veronica	1yr 3 months	13 Burrow Road	injured Tontine Street, died Royal Victoria Hospital	25th May 1917	daughter of Mr Frederick Sidney Holloway, merchants clerk

Horn	Edward	43	8 Radnor Cliffe, Sandgate	Station Approach Road	25th May 1917	butler to Sir Thomas Devitt of Radnor Cliffe, Sandgate
Houdart	Constant	33	99 Linden Crescent		25th May 1917	Belgian soldier
Hughes	Rose	34	46 Foord Road			spinster, school teacher
Jackman	Dorothy Bertha	14	12 Connaught Road	Tontine Street	25th May 1917	Daughter of Mr James Jackman, electrician
Jenner	Company Quarter Master Sergeant Oron Alfred	26	Shorncliffe Camp	Shorncliffe Camp	25th May 1917	Soldier in the 3rd Reserve Bn, Canadian Infantry, (Central Ontario Regt.). From Toronto Ontario.
Laxton	Katherine Euphemia	72	19 East Cliffe Gardens or East Street			widow
Lee	William		3 Marshland Road, New Eltham			general dealer, in Folkestone to make arrangements to take his donkeys to Dymchurch for the season
Lyth	Daniel Stringer	52	Craigside, Castle Road,	injured Hythe Churchyard, Hythe died Royal Victoria Hospital	25th May 1917	verger of Hythe Parish Church
Marchment	Jane	50	21 Manor Road	21 Manor Road	25th May 1917	cook to Mrs Callaghan, killed in the basement.
Maxted	Elizabeth	31	5 Grove Road		25th May 1917	wife of William Arthur Maxted, butcher's manager
McDonald	Agnes Curren	22	lodging at 12 Connaught Road, with Jackman family	injured Tontine Street, died Royal Victoria Hospital	1st June 1917	Canadian lady stenographer, waiting to proceed to France for ambulance work
McDonald	Albert Edward Charles	11	30 Stuart Road	Tontine Street	25th May 1917	son of Mr A Mc Donald, seaman, errand boy for Timothy Whites chemist in Tontine Street
McGuire	Ernest Henry	6	15 Linden Crescent	Tontine Street	25th May 1917	son of Mr Harry McGuire, marine fireman
Moss	Jane Charlotte	20	204 High Street Cheriton	Tontine Street	25th May 1917	wife of Pte George Moss, Labour Battalion
Moss	Walter George	2 mths	204 High Street Cheriton	Tontine Street	25th May 1917	son of Pte George Moss
Norris	Florence Kathleen	2	30 Blackbull Road	Tontine Street	25th May 1917	daughter of Alfred Norris, car mechanic
Norris	Florence Louise	24	30 Blackbull Road	Tontine Street	25th May 1917	wife of Alfred Norris, car mechanic
Norris	William Alfred John	10 mths	30 Blackbull Road	Tontine Street	25th May 1917	son of Alfred Norris, car mechanic
Reed	Mabel	12	37 Mead Road	injured Tontine Street, died Royal Victoria Hospital	25th May 1917	daughter of Mr Charles Reed, cabdriver
Robinson	John Walter Francis	6	64 St Michaels Street	Tontine Street	25th May 1917	son of John Robinson, a soldier
Rumsey	Florence (Florrie)	17	29 Blackbull Road	injured Tontine Street, died Royal Victoria Hospital	26th May 1917	daughter of Mr Rumsey, fish merchant, bookkeeper at Stokes Brothers
Stokes	Arthur Earnest	14	33a Harvey Street	injured Tontine Street, died Shorncliffe Military Hospital	28th May 1917	son of William Henry Stokes, greengrocer
Stokes	William Henry	46	33a Harvey Street	injured Tontine Street, died Royal Victoria Hospital	25th May 1917	greengrocer and fruiterer

Terry	Edith Gwendoline (Gwennie)	14	12 Connaught Road	Tontine Street	25th May 1917	school girl
Vane	Alfred	36	8 Bradstone New Road	Westcliffe Military Hospital	25th May 1917	jobbing gardener
Verschueren	Hyppolite	41	Sandgate Road	Tontine Street	25th May 1917	Belgian soldier at Staff Quarters
Walton	Doris Eileen Spencer	16	The Mount School, Julian Road	Athelstan Ladies School Shorncliffe Road	25th May 1917	school girl, home address 25 Bernard Gardens, Wimbledon
Waugh	Elizabeth Charlotte	48	47 Dover Road	Tontine Street	25th May 1917	wife of John Waugh, a soldier on foreign service
Wilson	Isabelle	80	11 East Street	Tontine Street	25th May 1917	widow of Mr James Wilson, gardener

APPENDIX K

PRIVATE PATRICK McHALE VC. Extract from the St George's Gazette 30 April 1894

We have much pleasure in placing before our readers, this short sketch of the life of Patrick McHale, VC, more especially, as hitherto all the previous "famous Fifth men" have been officers. There is no denying the fact that an officer has more opportunities of becoming "famous" as far as the outside world is concerned, but in the regiment, the memories and the gallant deeds of men like McHale and McManus will live for ever:

No 2626 Pat McHale, as he was generally called, enlisted for the 5th Fusiliers on December 18th, 1847. He was then 21 years old, and joined the Depot at Parkhurst Barracks, in the Isle of Wight.

Having passed his recruit's drill, he embarked for foreign service, on board the "Lady Edmondsbury," and sailed from Cowes on the following 8th of May. At this time McHale was a most powerful man, standing about six feet two inches, and with square shoulders and chest in proportion, he was what we may call a fine soldier; his complexion was fair, hair sandy, and his face much freckled. Pat was no scholar, he could neither read nor write. Soldiers were not then compulsorily obliged to attend the Regimental School, and many could not even sign their names to their accounts, but possibly Pat in after years attained to this degree of education. The following anecdote may be interesting to show that, in this early time of his soldiering, he possessed that indomitable will and pluck for which he was afterwards so distinguished; a voyage of three months in an old tub of a bark to the Mauritius was not like the pleasant and enjoyable passage it is to India now-a-days; the soldiers' rations were small and bad, and small as they were the men were frequently placed on short allowance -according to the state of the wind and weather - with the object of making them last till the end of the voyage. In addition to this, short weight was given whenever the third mate, who was deputed to issue the rations, could get the opportunity, the consequence was the Qr-Mr-Sergeant and the mate were at enmity. One morning after one of the frequent disputes as to short weight, the quarrel reached the upper deck, and the mate, losing his self control, rushed threateningly at the Sergeant to strike him; McHale who was standing by, placed himself in front of the mate, and with a determined look said, "Be Jabers, iv ye dare to lay a hand on him, I'll take ye by th' scruf o' th' neck and heave ye overboard." Pat's look and the words were enough, and the heaving overboard was dispensed with. Landing at the Mauritius on the 19th August, 1848, Pat served nine years in that beautiful island, doing his duty as a good and steady soldier.

Arriving with the Head Quarters of the Regiment in India, in 1857, he proceeded with his Company (Captain F W L'Estrange's) towards the North West Provinces, and was at the Relief of Arrah, and the operations in the Jugdeespoor District.

On the 3rd September, Pat, with the with his detachment, rejoined the Head Quarters, which had in the meantime arrived at Allahabad, and marched with it on the 5th towards Cawnpore, proceeding with Havelock's Column for the Relief of Lucknow Residency, he was present at the Battle of Mungulwar, the Capture of Alumbagh, and the Relief of Lucknow on the 25th September. In all these actions Pat was always to front, and, with-out fear for himself, performed valourous deeds with his bayonet, when the Sepoys would allow him to get near enough.

We have now arrived at the period when the Regiment was besieged for nearly two months in the Lucknow Residency. McHale shared cheerfully the hardships and privations of that time, and took part in various sallies, made for the purpose of capturing guns from the enemy, and clearing the surrounding houses and other obstacles too closely situated, which gave shelter to the mutineers. On the 2nd October, at the capture of the 'Cawnpore Battery', he was the first man to leap into the embrasure, and several of the Sepoy gunners were bayoneted by him.

On being relieved by Sir Colin Campbell in November, the Regiment was encamped at the Alumbagh, and was attached to the 1st Brigade of Sir James Outram's force. Here McHale found plenty of hard picquet duty, besides being almost constantly harassed by attacks of the enemy, but it was not until the 22nd December that an opportunity occurred for the display of his undaunted courage. Sir James Outram, through the medium of his spies, had heard that the mutineers were about to attack him in great force. In order to defeat this purpose he, in the dead of night, left his camp standing, and with the greater part of his force, proceeded to surprise the enemy who was bivouacked some two or three miles off the village of Guilee. Marching slowly in dead silence, and with unmeasured and broken tread, the force reached the village when a halt was made. At the outbreak of day Outram, in a loud voice, ordered the 'advance, the vedettes fired their carbines and bolted, the enemy found the English in their midst. Colonel Guy ordered the 'double', and as the Regiment cleared the street of the village and issued into an open space, it formed into line. While this movement was being completed, a gun belonging to the Sepoys, situated in a tope about 100 yards in front, was firing grape into it, and independent firing commenced as the companies formed up. No sooner was the Regiment in line, than the Colonel gave the order to 'charge', and away it went with a cheer at a steady 'double', but Pat with his usual impetuosity rushed in front, and alone bayoneted the gunners. When the main body arrived, Pat was attempting to turn the captured gun on the fleeing foe. For this act, together with his bravery at the 'Cawnpore Battery', McHale was unanimously elected by his comrades as one of the candidates for the VC – the number of these decorations to be given to the Regiment was limited to three, but there were others that deserved the distinction – the three fortunate recipients were elected by their fellows.

McHale was at the final capture of Lucknow, and also in the campaign in Oude in 1858-9. During all this time he was never absent from his duty for a single day, and it is almost wonderful to relate that he escaped without a single scratch.

Another anecdote will show the determined will of the man; the Regiment at Allalabad in 1859 was unfortunately visited by a severe epidemic of cholera, and Pat was one of the victims. A part of the treatment in those days was to strip the patient, and rub him violently all over with some kind of spirits. Pat was taken to Hospital, and when the Orderlies approached him with the object of carrying out this treatment, he would have none of it, but fought them with his fists and kept them from him. Although in great pain, he wildly patrolled the hospital ward during the whole night, and thus combated the disease. Pat was one of the very few attacked who escaped with their lives.

Returning to England in 1861, he served with the Regiment until it embarked for India in 1866, when he was sent with the rest of the old soldiers to Shorncliffe Regimental Depot.

In addition to having the Victoria Cross, he was in possession of the Mutiny Medal with clasps for the Defence of Lucknow, the Regimental Medal of Merit, and the Good Conduct Medal. He died at Shorncliffe on October 26th, 1866, and a stone, erected by his surviving comrades, marks the spot where rests the remains of as good and plucky a soldier as ever served in the ranks of the Fighting Fifth.

APPENDIX L
Regiments represented at Shorncliffe Military Cemetery

Principle Regiment	Including
Royal Artillery	Royal Horse Artillery, Garrison Artillery, Coastal Artillery, Royal Field Artillery and 1,3,4,9,11,18,25 and 43 Artillery Brigades
Queens Dragoon Guards	King's Dragoon Guards and 2 Dragoon Guards
Royal Scots Dragoon Guards	Scots Greys and 6 Dragoon Guards
Royal Dragoon Guards	4th and 7th Dragoon Guards
Queen's Royal Hussars	3rd, 4th, 7th and 8th Hussars

King's Royal Hussars	10th,11th,14th and 20th Hussars
Queen's Royal Lancers	5th,16th,17th and 21st Lancers
Royal Tank Regiment	Machine Gun Corps and Reconnaissance Regiment
Royal Engineers	Tunnelling, Works and Stevedore Regiments
Royal Signals	
Grenadier Guards	
Coldstream Guards	
Scots Guards	
Irish Guards	
Princess of Wales Royal Regiment	3rd,67th and 97th of Foot, West Surrey Regiment, West Kent Militia, Buffs, East Surrey Regiment, West Kent Regiment, Sussex Regiment, Middlesex Regiment, Hampshire Regiment and Queen's Regiment
King's Own Royal Border Regiment	4th, 34th and 55th of Foot, King's Own Royal Regiment and Border Regiment Militia
Royal Regiment of Fusiliers	Royal Northumberland Fusiliers, Warwickshire Fusiliers and the Royal Fusiliers
King's Regiment	8th and 96th of Foot and Manchester Regiment
Royal Anglian Regiment	9th,10th,12th, 16th,17th and 58th of Foot, Essex Regiment, Suffolk Regiment, Lincolnshire Regiment, Bedfordshire and Hertfordshire Regiment, Norfolk Regiment and Leicestershire Regiment
Devonshire and Dorset Regiment	11th of Foot, Dorset Regiment and Devonshire Regiment
The Light Infantry	Somerset Light Infantry, Duke of Cornwall's Light Infantry, King's Shropshire Light Infantry and Durham Light Infantry
Prince of Wales's Own Regiment of Yorkshire	Yorkshire Regiment, West Riding Regiment and West Yorkshire Rifles
Royal Highland Fusiliers	21st and 74th of Foot, Highland Light Infantry and Royal Scots Fusiliers
Cheshire Regiment	22nd of Foot and Cheshire Militia
Royal Welch Fusiliers	23rd of Foot
Royal Regiment of Wales	24th and 41st of Foot South Wales Borderers and Welch Regiment

King's Own Scottish Borderers

Royal Irish Regiment   83rd of Foot, Inniskilling Fusiliers, Royal Irish Fusiliers and Royal Irish Rifles

Royal Gloucester, Berkshire and Wiltshire Regiment   49th and 99th of Foot, Wiltshire Regiment and Duke of Edinburgh's Royal Regiment

Worcestershire and Sherwood Foresters Regiment   45th of Foot, Worcestershire Regiment and Sherwood Foresters

Queen's Lancashire Regiment   47th and 82nd of Foot, East Lancashire Regiment, South Lancashire Regiment and Lancashire Regiment

Duke of Wellington's   76th of Foot

Staffordshire Regiment   38th of Foot, South Staffordshire Regiment, North Staffordshire Regiment and Staffordshire Militia

Black Watch

The Highlanders   75th, 78th and 79th of Foot, the Gordons, Seaforths and Camerons

Argyll and Sutherland Highlanders   91st and 93rd of Foot

Parachute Regiment

Royal Green Jackets   52nd of Foot, 60th Rifles, Rifle Brigade, Oxfordshire and Buckinghamshire Light Infantry and King's Royal Rifle Corps

Small Arms School Corps   School of Musketry and Small Arms School, Hythe

Army Air Corps

Royal Logistics Corps   1st Battalion Military Train, Commissariat and Transport Corps, Army Service Corps, Chinese Labour Corps, Royal Army Service Corps, Royal Corps of Transport, Royal Army Ordnance Corps and Royal Pioneer Corps

Adjutant General's Corps   Army Hospital Corps, Medical Staff Corps, Royal Army Medical Corps, Military Foot Police, Mounted Police, Royal Army Pay Corps, Royal Army Education Corps and the Royal Army Chaplain Department

Royal Electrical and Mechanical Engineers

Queen Alexandra's Royal Nursing Corps

Intelligence Corps

Auxiliary Territorial Service,
Women's Royal Army Corps,
Kent Cyclists, 100 (Canadian)
Regiment
City of Dublin Regiment and
Militia and Royal Dublin Fusiliers

Selected Bibliography and Sources

Napoleon, Master of Europe, by Alistair Horne.

La Grande Armee by Georges Blond.

Bonaparte by Corelli Barnett.

Britain Against Napoleon, by Carola Oman.

Napoleon at the Channel, by Carola Oman.

Dumouriez and the Defence of England against Napoleon by Holland Rose and Broadley.

Napoleon at the Boulogne Camp by F. Nicolay.

Years of Endurance 1793-1802, by Arthur Bryant.

Years of Victory 1802-1812, by Arthur Bryant.

Kent in the Napoleonic Wars, by Peter Bloomfield.

The Road to Waterloo, Ed. Alan J.Guy (National Army Museum).

The Oxfordshire and Buckinghamshire Light Infantry, by Philip Booth.

The Story of the Oxfordshire and Buckinghamshire Light Infantry, by Sir Henry Newbolt.

Recollections of an Old 52nd Man, by Captain John Dobbs.

The Dorset Rifleman, Ed. Eileen Hathaway.

History of the War in the Peninsula, Vol 1, by W.F.P.Napier.

Sir John Moore, by Carola Oman.

The Life of Sir John Moore, by James Carrick Moore.

Sir John Moore's System of Training, by J.F.C.Fuller.

The Diary of Sir John Moore, by J.F.Maurice.

Pitt the Younger by Derek Jarrett.

The War Speeches of William Pitt, selected by R.Coupland.

Sunlight and Shadow by John B.Gough.

Autobiography and Personal Recollections of John B. Gough.

Rural Rides by William Cobbett.

Excursions in the County of Kent, 1822.

Pride and Prejudice by Jane Austen.

Charles Dickens in Folkestone, by C.H.Bishop.

The School of Musketry at Hythe, by W.S.Miller.

Hand-Book for Hythe, by Hans Busk.

The History of Hythe Ranges, by Dougie Maber.

A Brief History of The Small Arms Corps and The Small Arms Wing, School of Infantry, Hythe, by Captain A.J. Parsons MBE.

Folkestone During the War 1914-1919, by Rev J.C.Carlisle.

Folkestone and the War, by Councillor John Jones.

Somme, by Lynn MacDonald.

Seek Glory, Now Keep Glory, by John Ashby.

Flying, The First World War in Kent, by David Collyer.

The Tigers, by Matthew Richardson.

A Short History of 3rd The King's Own Hussars by Lieutenant-Colonel F.R. Burnside.

Folkestone, the Story of a Town by C.H.Bishop.

A Saunter Through Kent (various) by Charles Igglesdon.

Hythe Haven, by Duncan Forbes.

The Barracks Act of 1890, by Roy Brook (MA Thesis, University of Wales).

Bygone Kent, Published by Meresborough Books, various articles.

Talking History No 1 by Folkestone and District Local History Society.

The Fynmore Scrapbooks at Folkestone Library.

Martello Towers, by Sheila Sutcliffe.

The Journal of the Army Historical Research Society, Vol 27, 1949.

Flood, Fire and Sudden Death in Old Hythe, by Denise Rayner.

The Royal Military Canal, by P.A.L.Vine.

Mercenaries for the Crimea, by C.C.Bayley.

Costume of the Army of the British Empire, by Charles Hamilton Smith.

The East Kent Mounted Rifles by R.J. Smith.

Social Life in England by John Finnemore.

English Social History by G.M.Trevelyan.

Shorncliffe Military Cemetery by Colonel P.R.S.Jackson, O.B.E.

A Short History of Shorncliffe Garrison edited by Lieutenant Colonel (Retired) J.C. Caverhill.

Sandgate, The Rise and Progress of a Village, by Linda Rene-Martin.

The Register of the Victoria Cross.

A Widow-Making War, The Life and Death of a British Officer in Zululand, 1879. Ed. Howard Whitehouse.

Ladysmith by Ruari Chisholm.

ABOUT THE AUTHORS

Father and son, Michael and Martin George have lived in Folkestone for over 20 years. A keen interest in history and a curiosity about Shorncliffe Camp led to a three-year collaboration resulting in this book. With a mix of traditional research techniques and with the aid of the internet they have produced this comprehensive social and military history of the Kent coast between Folkestone, Hythe and the Romney Marsh.

After leaving school, Michael spent two years in the Metropolitan Police, leaving to study law at university. He qualified as a solicitor in 1977 and has worked in local government and private practice. Since 1990 he has been a Crown Prosecutor handling a number of high profile criminal cases.

Martin is studying for a Masters Degree in law at the University of Nottingham and intends to pursue a career in the law, but hopes to have time to continue with his interest in history.